Running Christian Groups in Schools

Running Christian Groups in Schools

Esther Bailey

Scripture Union

Scripture Union, 207–209 Queensway, Bletchley, MK2 2EB, England.

First published 1998

ISBN 1 85999 199 8

British Library Cataloguing-in-Publication Data
A catalogue record for this book is available from the British Library.

Cover design by Blue Pig Design Company.
Illustrations by Dan Donovan.

Printed and bound in Great Britain by Ebenezer Baylis & Son Limited, The Trinity Press, Worcester and London.

CONTENTS

1

WHY GO INTO SCHOOLS TO RUN CHRISTIAN GROUPS?

I grew up in a Christian family, in a church that was based in our own home. There was certainly no shortage of Bible teaching and Christian example around. However, it was only when I joined the Christian Union at secondary school (there was no club at my primary school) that I became involved, for the first time, in putting my faith into action. I was praying about things that mattered to me, about activities I was involved in. And I discovered, staggeringly, that God actually answered! Of course, I knew in theory that God always answers prayer, but this was the first time I discovered for myself that he listens to and answers *me*.

When I began teaching, I started running a Christian club myself. Some of the children came because they had Christian parents who encouraged them to attend. But most came because they were bored and had nothing else to do. And they met God!

There was so much to learn from those children. They didn't know the 'right answers', and they forced me to think about what I was really saying, what I really believed.

A few years ago I met up with one of those children again. He had become a student teacher, he was still following Jesus, and he was keen to set up a Christian group in his school once he started teaching.

As a Scripture Union schools worker, I have been running a Christian club in a local school for a number of years. One young boy who came along really intrigued me: it was difficult to work out why he bothered. He was the only boy in an otherwise all-girls club. He wasn't particularly friendly to any of the girls; in fact he was mostly extremely rude to them. He didn't come from a Christian family. His first visit to a church was on a club outing to something that just happened to take place in a church building. He was aggressive, used colourful language, was often disruptive and frequently got into trouble. Yet he kept on coming.

He had been part of the club for three and a half years, when we started doing a series on people who followed Jesus. One session was about people who follow Jesus today. I had a couple of visitors with me that week, and we decided to talk about our own faith, 'interviewing' each other about how we started following Jesus and why, what was good about it, what was hard about it, and so on. As we chatted, Lee suddenly joined in, talking about his own experiences. Even though I hadn't seen much evidence in his life, he had been following Jesus. The school-based club was his only support and source of teaching.

Lee has now moved on to another school where there is no Christian club, but his younger sister has started coming to the one I run. I wonder if he is still following Jesus. I pray that God will keep hold of him.

These three stories illustrate some of the reasons why school-based groups are useful.

Putting faith into practice

A school-based club gives children from Christian families the opportunity to meet with other Christians from different backgrounds and different denominations. It gives them the chance to explore what they believe. They may take on responsibilities in the group such as helping to set up or clear away, praying for the other children and the group leader, doing assemblies as part of the group and getting involved in projects both in the local and wider community. All these things will help the children make up their minds whether or not they consciously want to opt into the faith in which they have been brought up, to be thinking Christians with their own set of beliefs rather than just clones of their parents.

Children with no church contact

Perhaps more importantly in a society where 86 per cent of children have no contact with a church, a school-based Christian club may provide the only opportunity some will have to hear that God loves them and wants to be in relationship with them. There is no guarantee that RE lessons or assemblies will actually contain Christian teaching, and for some children the name of Jesus may only be heard as a swear word. Although many do have a vague concept of God, often their understanding is narrow or warped. The club could provide the setting where they are challenged to come to a real understanding of who God is.

Planting spiritual seeds

Although children may learn about God, it is unlikely you will see many conversions or much spiritual fruit in a school Christian club. Children come for a short time, some perhaps only for a couple of weeks before they move on. Much of the value of the group is in planting seeds in the children's minds, through stories and examples of Christian people, through discussions which help them apply truths to their lives, through the memory verses and songs they learn. It is up to God then to water and nurture those seeds and perhaps bring them to maturity.

Recently I was feeling discouraged, wondering whether there was any point in continuing with a club that seemed to be getting nowhere. Over the course of the next couple of months, I happened to hear the testimonies of a number of people who had become Christians in their thirties, forties or fifties. All of them mentioned that when, as adults, they had felt God begin to draw them to himself, they remembered things they had heard as children, things they had learnt at Sunday school or in Scripture lessons at school, things that a Christian friend had said. God was reassuring me about the role of the school club, and confirming that he would decide how his work would continue in the lives of the children who came.

Children from non-Christian families

A school-based club might attract children who would never, or could never, come to church. Primary school children are generally still very dependent on their parents. If the parents do not go to church, or do not support their child's wish to go, it is very unlikely he will become a regular member of a Sunday group. Sundays hold so many other attractions these days: shopping has become a very popular activity; a lot of sport for children takes place then; it is a day for family outings; and children of divorced couples often spend weekends away from home with the parent who does not live with them. The attraction of school as a place for the club is that the children are there anyway, and they are on familiar territory. By contrast, a church venue may seem threatening and scary.

Christian witness in school

A school-based club may encourage various kinds of Christian witness in the school. Often I meet teachers who see the need for a Christian group and feel guilty because they personally cannot become involved due to other pressures and commitments. When the club is run by parents, governors, dinner ladies, secretaries or whoever, the teacher is free to be a Christian influence in other areas of school life. The club can offer to take assemblies or undertake practical tasks around the school. All these things raise the profile of Christians within the school. A school-based club is a witness to everyone who works or studies there, not just to the children who come.

Salt and light

Jesus said, 'You are like salt ... You are like light' (Matt 5:13–14). Salt is something that permeates its environment: in cooking it is more often noticed by its absence than its presence. Light, on the other hand, is something that is apparent straightaway. A school Christian club offers the opportunity to be both salt and light. The role of light can be discerned in the teaching aspect of the club, where the children are told directly about God. But the salt role takes effect during the time spent in building relationships with the children and letting them see the Christian faith lived out. Perhaps, as Christians, we recognise the value of 'light-type' activities more than 'salty' ones; but both are necessary when working with children (and sometimes teachers) who know absolutely nothing about God.

Another extracurricular activity

Some schools would love children to have the opportunity of another extracurricular club, and so would be very grateful to you for offering your services. However, others may be very suspicious of your motives. In either case, it is important to talk through your programme beforehand with the head-teacher.

A word about church-based clubs

Though this book is aimed at clubs based in schools, much of the advice will be equally useful if you run a midweek, church-based club. There are a number of reasons for choosing to run a club in a church rather than a school setting.

Use of resources

In a church-based club you will probably know what

resources are available to you. In a school this may be more difficult to establish or reach agreement on.

CONTINUITY

Continuity is sometimes easier to maintain in a church-based club. School clubs have to stop for the school holidays, and contact is lost when children move on to different schools.

OPENING DOORS

A club run in a church may open the door for a child and her family to come to other church services and maybe, eventually, to join in the full life of the church. Although children may become Christians in a school-based club, they will still have to make quite an adjustment before they can feel familiar with church culture.

FINDING HELPERS

On a practical note, it may be easier to find helpers for an early evening church-based club, than for a school-based one which has to fit into the lunch-break or the late afternoon.

Finally...

Wherever your work with children is based, I hope that this book will help you think through what you are doing and why, so that many more children have the opportunity to hear that God loves them and wants to be their friend.

2

AIMS AND EXPECTATIONS

One of the things that struck me most forcibly when I started working with Scripture Union and visiting different Christian groups in schools was that there was no such thing as a typical group. Look, for example, at the *raison d'être* of each of the following four groups:

- *Group 1* had been started by a school secretary who was worried about the children being bored during the lunch-hour and wanted to give them something constructive to do.

- *Group 2* was a sort of nurture group for some children who had gone forward at an evangelistic meeting.

- *Group 3* was trying to replace a Sunday school that had dwindled away to hardly anything.

- *Group 4* was an attempt to get children interested in developing-world issues and raising money for Tear Fund.

As you start running a group, it is important that you are clear in your mind why you are doing so and what you hope to achieve. It is also good to review your aims regularly, perhaps on an annual basis. You might think through questions like these:

- Are the reasons for starting the group still good enough for keeping it going?

- Is what you are doing the best way of working towards your aims?

- Do your aims need to change?

As you consider what purpose the group is serving, you might decide that you could achieve more by a change of emphasis. For instance, the 'nurture' group mentioned above remained relevant only as long as those particular children came to the group. Once new members joined and the original members left for other schools, the group had to change its approach. The secretary with the lunch-time club needed to make her aims more specific as she started to plan what it might do each week. And the group raising money for Tear Fund discovered that while this was all right for a short-term project, it was not the basis for a term-in, term-out, year-in, year-out Christian group in the school.

Of course, you will not be the only one involved in deciding the aims of the group. The children who come, the school and the local church may all have widely differing expectations! For example, you may feel that your main aim is to help children understand that God loves them and wants to be their friend. However, it is very unlikely that the children will come for this reason! They are far more likely to attend because they think the club will be fun. So, to achieve your aim, you will have to make it fun.

In the first group I ran as a teacher, I discovered that the children were coming along to play games. If we had a game at the beginning of the session, a number of children would 'have to catch the bus' or 'need to be home by such and such a time' as soon as the 'God bits' of the programme started. When I moved the game to the end, I found that they arrived later and later, in time for the game but not much else. I soon realised that I needed to provide a varied programme so that the children could not predict week to week when the games session might be. Sometimes we had two games sessions, and sometimes – when I was really inspired – we even got the teaching across through the game! I felt that it was important to meet the children's expectations to a certain extent: for some it was their only contact with God and it would have been awful if that contact was a disappointing experience. But, at the same time, I was reluctant to give in completely to their desires, as this would have meant not achieving the aims I had for the group. I needed to strike the right balance.

The club may be influenced not only by the expectations of those who attend but also of those who don't. You may find it worthwhile to consider what sort of image the club has within the school.

It may be very positive, and there may be children wishing they could come. But sometimes, for some reason, a club has a negative image, with the result that club members are teased by their peers. A club in a local school recently got the reputation of being only for girls and, try as they might, the leaders could not persuade boys to come. Eventually the club was stopped for a term, then relaunched with a different name. Now over one-third of the members are boys, and its image is quite different.

The school's expectations of the club also need to be considered very carefully. The club can only exist with the permission of the head-teacher, and it is very important to be sure that she understands and agrees with your aims. It is good to make a point each term of explaining (briefly) to the head what your programme will be. If there are criticisms of the group from either staff or parents, it is likely that she will be the person to deal with them. Complaints are more likely to be dealt with sympathetically if the head feels confident that she knows what you are doing in the club.

On a practical level, all sorts of misunderstandings can be avoided by finding out if the school considers the Christian group to be part of their extracurricular programme or an independent event using the school premises.

The local church may or may not be aware of the group's existence, and you will need to decide whether or not you want to approach it. The church may have a real concern for the school, and be very encouraged to hear of your club. Church members may be able to provide prayer support for you and possibly even help run it. If so, it is vital that you spend time with the church, sharing your vision and explaining your aims. Otherwise, it could join in enthusiastically only to withdraw later, disappointed not to have gained more children for church activities through the work in the school. Ideally, the church should see the school group as valuable in its own right, not as a means to the end of recruiting for a Sunday school.

A local church can do a lot to support a club in a school, such as encouraging children of church members to join, releasing parents from other church responsibilities so that they have time to help, subsidising the cost of training for the leaders, providing resources, and praying for the club and its witness within the school.

Finally...

Maybe it is stating the obvious, but it is worth thinking about what God's expectations are of the group and of you as a leader. Once the group has been running for some time, God may be saying things like 'It's time for you to have a break', or 'This group has served its purpose – it's time for it to stop now', or 'I want you to change and do things differently'. We need to take time to listen to his guiding words.

3

WHO WILL RUN THE GROUP?

School employees

Traditionally, Christian groups in schools were run by a Christian teacher. This is an easy relationship as far as the school is concerned: the teacher, or other employee (secretary, dinner lady or caretaker, for instance), is known by the school and the school is likely to be less suspicious of their motives for wanting to run the group. An employee of the school will know what resources are available and be able to negotiate for the group to use them. Running a Christian group may be seen as a valid part of the employee's work for the school. On the other hand, it may be treated as something the individual has chosen to do in their own time, on top of their normal workload.

Volunteers

These days more and more schools are encouraging volunteers (usually parents of pupils) to get involved in extracurricular activities. If the group is run by volunteers, the head-teacher will need to have confidence that they are suitable and responsible people. Quite likely, individual volunteers will be asked to sign a form declaring they have no criminal convictions – this should not be taken to indicate lack of trust or opposition to the Christian nature of the group.

Joint leadership

This may combine the best of both worlds: a couple of people – one an employee of the school, the other a volunteer – lead the group together. The employee knows the school, knows the children and has confidence in dealing with them. The volunteer, on the other hand, may carry the bulk of the preparation and organisation.

Churches working together

A number of churches in an area may choose to get involved in the work of a single school group. (This is a good way to develop the Christian community through increasing fellowship, and provides an opportunity to sort out any misunderstandings.) It is important to discuss what each church's input might be, and what its expectations are, beforehand. For example, one church might want to advertise its holiday club to the members of the school group. Would the other churches be happy for that to happen, or would it be regarded as unfair 'poaching'?

Team leadership

If there is a team of people running the group, you will need to sort out whether to have one overall leader or to share responsibilities on a rota system. If different people take responsibility for different areas, who is going to coordinate things?

Do not automatically assume that everyone involved is there for the same reasons! You should spend time making sure that you do all share a common vision for the group. One big advantage of team leadership is that you can encourage each other to pray regularly for the work. One person on his own may find that prayer time is pushed aside by all the things clamouring to be done. But a team who sets aside time to pray won't be able to forget to pray! However, you will need to consider what the team will do if things go wrong. If there are disagreements, how will they be handled?

Calling

We must always remember that the group is God's work. Some people who lead groups do have a clear sense that God is calling them to that task. Others may start a group because the vicar, a friend, the head-teacher, their children or someone else asked them to start it. God may well be speaking through such people, but the organiser will need to work out if leading the group is really the role God means him to have. (Of course, God does often ask us just to use our common sense and get on with what needs doing!)

I remember going through a crisis of my own over whether or not I should be leading a particular school group. Most of the children came from broken homes and had been quite hurt by life. I felt that, coming from a stable background with parents, a husband and friends who loved me, I was not perhaps the best person to run this particular group. What right had I to share God's love with children who did not believe that *anyone* loved them?

Then one day I went to do an assembly in an infants' school. The hymn the music-teacher had chosen was 'There is peace like a river in my soul'. It carries on, 'There is love … There is joy…' In the afternoon I visited another school club. An elderly lady came in regularly to play the piano, and the hymn she practised for that week was 'Peace is flowing like a river / Flowing out to you and me / Spreading out into the desert / Setting all the captives free'. Verse two began 'Love is flowing…' and verse three began 'Joy is flowing…' That evening I went to my own church's prayer-meeting. The first song we sang was 'Peace I give to you', with verses two and three beginning – you've guessed it! – with 'Love' and 'Joy'.

Coincidence? I really felt that God was saying, 'You know my peace, love and joy – you must let these things flow out to the children so that they can be set free.' I carried on running the group!

We're all visual aids

Some people are daunted by the thought of being a group leader and feel quite unable to take an up-front role. However, all Christians who are involved in the group, whether in a major or a very minor way, are being 'visual aids' for God. Much of what the children learn about God will come not from the Bible stories you teach but from the way you treat them – whether you take an interest in them, how much trouble you take to get to know them. This can be quite a frightening thought – we are all aware of what poor visual aids we must be at times – but it is also encouraging to realise that however gifted or ungifted we feel, we are a vital part of the spiritual input just by being there!

> We who are strong in the faith ought to help the weak … in order to build them up in the faith … Everything written in the Scriptures was written … that we might have hope through the patience and encouragement which the Scriptures give us. And may God, the source of patience and encouragement, enable you to have the same point of view among yourselves by following the example of Christ Jesus…
>
> *Romans 15:1–5, GNB*

4

SETTING UP THE GROUP

If you feel God is telling you to start a group in your local school, the first and most important thing to do is to pray!

- Pray that God will prepare the way for you to go into the school, and that he will make the staff receptive to the idea of a group.
- Pray that he will bring together the right people to lead the group.
- Pray that he will make it clear to you what he wants as the decisions are being made.
- Pray for all the children who will come to the group. God knows each of them already and is far more aware than we are of their needs and desires.

Contacting the school

The group will only exist at the discretion of the head-teacher, so it is important to discuss things with her at an early stage. If you know the head, the obvious way forward would be to phone and ask for an appointment to meet and talk your ideas through. If you do not know the head personally, it may be better to write, outlining your ideas and giving some sort of accreditation: whether you have run this sort of group before or have visited a school where a similar group was running successfully; whether you have had any relevant training; whether someone known to the head could vouch for you. Follow up your letter with a phone call, asking to meet and discuss things further.

It is important to establish certain basics, such as whether the club is covered by the school's public liability insurance policy, or whether you have permission to use its resources (eg the television and video, the photocopier, games equipment, scissors) and if so, whether or not you have to contribute towards costs. It would also be helpful to know whether the room you use is ever likely to be needed for something else during club-time, and what the system is for clearing away craft activities and such like.

Make contact early with the caretaker. He or she will need to reorganise cleaning rotas or arrange locking up if your group is to be held in a classroom after school. (A supportive caretaker will be a great help when you can't find the video remote control, or you want to borrow the set of Bibles normally kept in the library.)

And, of course, get in touch with the teaching staff. It is a matter of courtesy to keep them informed. Practically, you will want to avoid clashing with other extracurricular activities and to keep on good negotiating terms (for example, on how indoor space is allocated when the weather is wet).

Getting support

As mentioned earlier, local churches can provide support for a school club through prayer, finance, manpower and encouragement.

There may be elderly or housebound folk who would pray regularly for the club and for you as you lead it. Perhaps you could give them the names of individual children once the group has got under way.

As far as finance is concerned, the school may have a small amount of money to allocate to extracurricular clubs. Some local authorities or educational charities give a grant for this sort of project, for either buying resources or training leaders. Find ways of getting resources for free, or at least as cheaply as possible (see the 'Resources' section for ideas). Investigate whether local church Sunday groups would be willing to lend you videos occasionally – since your group meets on a weekday, you are unlikely to need them at the same time as the Sunday group.

Who?

Fairly early on, you will need to decide who the group is for. Will it be open to all the children in the school, or will membership be limited to just one or two year groups? Your decision will be influenced by the number of helpers available, the size of the school, the current practice with other clubs in the school, and how confident you feel about working with a particular age group.

Limiting the age range makes it easier to provide appropriate activities. Of course, if you have lots of help, you can separate children into different age groups. Some clubs are only open to the top two years in the school, making them something the children look forward to being able to join. Others start with the bottom two years of the school and extend the age range each year.

It may be necessary to decide how many children the club can comfortably contain. One group in an infants' school, which had been meeting for twenty minutes in a lunch-break, had seventy children attending. The leaders decided they really could not cope with that many children, so, during the following term, half the children came for the first half of the term and the rest for the second half.

When?

As far as possible, the Christian group should be regarded in the same way as the school's other extracurricular activities. If these tend to take place after school, it would be better for the group to be after school rather than at lunch-time (or vice versa). If the school offers activities both at lunch-time and after school, you may have more choice.

Lunch-time clubs have the advantage that the children who want to are all able to come – those who share lifts with others, or who have to go home by bus, are not left out. And any parents who want to help are still able to lead a group without their children having to attend if they don't choose to. However, lunch-times are sometimes very rushed and there may not be time to do very much. And a teacher running a lunch-time group may find that he goes all through the day without a break.

It is important to know which other clubs are likely to be running at the same time as yours. In a busy school there are bound to be clashes, but, with a bit of research, you can minimise the effects of these. If the group is intended for children from Years 5 and 6, it would be unwise to run it at the same time as the Year 5 and 6 football club. However, having it at the same time as the lower-school choir should not cause too many problems!

If the group is meeting after school, you will need to decide how long the sessions should be. As a general rule, it is better to go for a shorter time than you think you can comfortably fill. It will be less stressful to finish a session thinking that there was more you could have done, than to spend the last few minutes panicking about what on earth to do. Of course, if you really find that the time you have allocated is just not long enough, you can always extend it. This would be far more positive than having to make the sessions shorter.

Where?

If you are a volunteer coming into the school to run the group, the head-teacher will probably suggest where you might meet. You may be offered the canteen, the school hall or a classroom space. Think carefully about the activities you want to include in the programme. If you are going to play lots of games, a large area – such as the canteen, the hall or access to an outside playground – will be important. If craft activities are going to predominate, a classroom may be more suitable. However, if you are running the group in a classroom and you are not the class-teacher, you will need to work at building a good relationship with the person who is. Make sure you leave the classroom as you found it (you may want to move the desks aside for the duration of the club). Finish on time, especially at lunch-time, and be ready to leave quickly.

A name for the group

You may like to think of a name for your group in the planning stages. Some groups start without one and allow the children to choose (though you then run the risk that they decide on something unsuitable!). Having a name beforehand certainly helps when you are advertising the group.

Choose something that sounds fun but also reflects the Christian aspect of the group: Lighthouse, Explorers, Adventurers and Find-Outers are all popular. Often children like names that are acrostics – JAM (Jesus And Me), JUMP (Jesus Understands Me Perfectly) or JAFFA (Jesus, A Friend For All) Kids. A name indicating the day of meeting – Friday Club – will help the children remember when the club is. Avoid a name that has Christian connotations but which is beyond the child's understanding. One boy, who went regularly to a Quest Club, kept asking the teacher when they were going to play the game. She was not sure what he meant because they played games most weeks. Eventually she realised that he thought he had joined the Chess Club and, although he was enjoying what was happening each week, he was waiting to play chess!

Contacting the home

Children are individuals, but they are also part of families which may or may not be sympathetic to the aims of your group. Misunderstandings can easily arise at home if the group leader is not sensitive to the home situation. Some children may be of other faiths. A proportion will come from homes with two parents who are married to each other; but in some areas very few children will have any experience of such a home.

In a primary school, children attend clubs voluntarily but only with parental permission. When the group starts, you may like to send a letter home with every child in the school, explaining what its aims are and what the programme each week is likely to include. This letter should contain a tear-off slip for parents to sign, giving permission for their child to attend the group. Find out whether the school expects this permission to be reissued each term, or whether it may be done annually. After the launch of the club, information about your group may be included in a general letter about all school clubs. You may feel that this is sufficient, or you may like to send fuller information to parents of new children.

Advertising

If children are going to come to the group, particularly when it is just starting, you will have to let them know what it is about. A good way is to ask to take an assembly: you will probably get to speak to all the children together. A lively interesting presentation involving the children and ending with the punch-line 'If you enjoyed that and would like to know more, come along to…' will usually generate interest. It is useful if your plug in assembly takes place on the same day as you send letters home to parents; then children will have some idea whether or not they want permission to attend.

Bright posters placed strategically around the school, and a message sent round the classes, will remind the children when the group is about to start.

Getting the group to take assembly once a term or once a year may attract new members.

Existing members can be encouraged to invite friends along personally.

5

PRINCIPLES OF PROGRAMME PLANNING

When starting to plan a programme for a club, you need to bear in mind the needs of the children who might come, the abilities of the leaders and, as we considered earlier in 'Setting up the group', the potential/limitations of where you are to meet.

The children

Ages

Having decided which age group(s) the club is aimed at, leaders need to make sure they understand the problems and possibilities this presents. Infant-age children (5–7s) think concretely and take language literally. They may be very worried by the thought of Jesus 'living in someone's heart' and are more likely to understand Jesus as their friend than as their Lord. Lower-junior children (7–9s) are often hero-worshippers, and they will probably respond best to the idea of Jesus as a king. They also like to be part of a gang, so joining Jesus' gang would appeal to them. Upper-junior children (9–11s) are beginning to think abstractly and will be able to discuss what might happen in hypothetical situations. They are likely to come up with some tough questions (which will need serious answers).

Abilities

Leaders also need to take account of the abilities of the particular children who come to the group. Those who struggle academically would be discouraged if they had to do a lot of reading or writing. For them, a wordsearch or crossword would be torture; whereas a word-based activity may be a treat for a bright child. Children who shine at sport would welcome the inclusion of games in the programme, but those who don't may be made to feel failures. Artistic children enjoy craft activities. Some children love singing; others hate it! Obviously, it will take time to get to know the preferences of everyone, and there may be clashes of interest. As far as possible, the programme should contain a variety of activities and change from week to week.

Backgrounds

Some school groups consist mainly of children from Christian families; some are made up entirely of children from unchurched families; and some contain children from other faith groups. Each case means taking a different starting point. For instance, it will make a difference to the way a Bible story is told if it is familiar to the children or completely new. (For ways to tell Bible stories, see pp 21–22.)

Behaviour

While a few Christian groups have no behaviour problems, most leaders find their groups 'lively', and some groups seem to attract all the school's delinquents! Bear in mind which category your group falls into when you plan activities. Will a particular game work, or will it be a riot? Will a craft activity be an appropriate reinforcement of a teaching point, or is it likely to result in the 'redecoration' of the classroom?

Sometimes the group's behaviour depends on whether one particular child attends. There may be a couple of children who clash endlessly if they are both there. This sort of group dynamic is very hard to plan around if you do not know from week to week who will come. It may be useful to plan lots of group work, separating children who clash with each other or who form an unholy alliance. If one child dominates in a negative way, plan activities where you can work alongside that child and give her lots of positive attention. (See pp 27–30 on handling problems.)

Content

Finally, when thinking about the needs of the children, the leaders should be aware of the teaching they want to get across. If the group is the children's only Christian contact, are they receiving a balanced picture of what God is like and what it means to be his friend? Have their ideas about God changed since they started coming to the group? How else can you help them make spiritual progress?

The leaders

When putting together a programme, it is important to assess the strengths and weaknesses of the leadership team, and to plan in such a way as to maximise the former and compensate for the latter. If you enjoy doing something, it will come across to the children far more positively than if you are just doing it because you feel you have to. If you are part of a team of leaders, discuss together what each of you feels are your strengths, such as leading the games, teaching, getting alongside individual children, organising drinks and biscuits. Work out how you can each take turns at doing the things you enjoy. If you hate craft work, or if telling stories in front of all the children terrifies you, then don't! Leave it to someone else.

Carry out this team assessment regularly, perhaps once a term. Someone new may join and feel able to do only one or two things at first. However, as he grows in confidence he may be willing to take on more. Equally, someone who has had a high profile role may want to withdraw for a bit and do less.

If you are leading the group on your own, you may have to look elsewhere to compensate for your areas of weakness. Perhaps there is a local schools worker or church-based children's worker who could visit, possibly once a term, and take the group. Or you may find that the areas you consider to be weaknesses can be overcome by training. Find out if there are any suitable training courses that may help.

Where you meet

The final thing to consider when planning your programme is where the group is to be held (see p 16, and also 'Games' on p 24).

6

PROGRAMME PLANNING

This section looks at the specifics of programme planning and deals in turn with the various components that may make up the programme. You may find it helpful to use a ready-made programme outline, such as *On Track*, a booklet produced by Scripture Union in Schools each term, for people running groups in primary schools. However, no published material is going to suit your group all the time: it will need adapting to fit your situation and should be regarded as a starting point rather than the answer to all your programme-planning problems!

Using the Bible with children

These days it certainly can't be taken for granted that there will be a Bible in every home. Yet many children are fascinated when they get the chance to read stories about Jesus in the Bible for themselves. Recently I did a mini-survey, asking children in the schools I visited whether any of them had ever read anything from the Bible. In every school, I discovered that a handful of children had picked up the Bible just out of curiosity and started reading it. Without any support or explanation, some had read from Genesis right through to the Prophets, or from Matthew through to the Pauline Epistles. If children want to find out what the Bible is about, we need to look for ways in which to encourage them. I felt sad that some children had read so much and then given up, disappointed. With the right guidance and encouragement, they could have been helped to understand the relevance of the Bible to their lives.

When using the Bible with children, bear in mind that not every child will be able to read it; they may be too young or not have the necessary academic ability or skills. Choose a simple translation, such as the *Contemporary English Version* or the *Good News Bible*, and use passages that are relevant to the children. The leader could read a short portion once or twice, then let the children respond to what they have heard by modelling in play-dough, or drawing, or playing musical instruments.

Often adults pre-digest Bible passages and feed the children bland snippets, never bringing them into contact with the Bible itself. We should not be afraid of allowing God to speak directly to children through his word. However, we do need to ensure that we are introducing them to suitable passages in manageable sections, and giving support when it is required.

When preparing to use a passage with children, ask yourself questions like:

- Why was this passage included in the Bible?
- What might God have been saying to people through this passage at the time it was written?
- What might he be saying to people today?
- In what areas of the children's lives would this passage be relevant?
- How can I help these children discover, in an exciting way, what God is saying through this passage?

Answering questions like these will help you choose methods that will engage the children in a relevant way without distorting the truth of God's word or taking things out of context.

Storytelling

Probably the best way to introduce children to the Bible is through the medium of storytelling. A good story, well-told, will grip their attention and fire their imaginations. The following are tried and tested principles for good storytelling:

- Prepare thoroughly and make sure you know the facts. Even if it is a story you are very familiar with, go back to the Bible and read the original version: with a story that is told often, it is quite possible that the embellishments and poetic licence have become more important than the original facts.

- Think about how to approach the story. Will it be in first person, or third (I or he)? Will it be in the present tense, as if it were actually happening as the story unfolds; or will it be in the past? Can it be told from an unusual point of view? For example, the story of Zacchaeus could be told by Zacchaeus himself, by one of the disciples, by someone in the crowd who paid his taxes to Zacchaeus, by a servant in Zacchaeus' house, or even by the sycamore tree or a bird nesting in it. What sort of introduction will get the children's attention? How will it end?

- Involve the children as much as possible. The more of their senses you use, the more they will remember. As well as listening, they will need things to see and do.

- Visual aids should be clear and easy for every child to see. Remember that you are also a visual aid: if you look bored, the children will think the story is boring; if you look excited, they will think it is exciting. Use facial expressions, gestures and posture to your advantage.

- Think how you can involve the other senses. For example, when telling the story of Jacob and Esau, have feely-bags containing rough and smooth things. When telling the story of feeding the five thousand, pass around bits of sardine sandwich for the children to eat. Spray some perfume into the air when telling the story of the woman who washed Jesus' feet.

  If you are telling the story of Gideon, divide half the children into three groups. Have the other half lie down in the middle of the room and pretend to be asleep. The three groups creep into position and then, on your signal, shout, 'A sword for the Lord and for Gideon!'

- Ask the children to act out a story in small groups.

- Stop at a crucial point in the story to vote on what they think might come next. For example, when Joseph recognises his brothers in Egypt, ask the children if they think Joseph will punish his brothers for what they did to him. Who thinks he will keep quiet and not tell them who he is? Who thinks he will forgive them? Then go on to tell the rest of the story and show who got it right.

- Teach the children actions that they have to do whenever you use certain words. For example, in the story of Daniel, they could put their hands on their hearts every time Daniel is mentioned; bow every time the king is mentioned; growl every time the lions are mentioned; cheer every time God is mentioned.

- Have a definite purpose for telling the story. There must be some link between the story and the child's world today. Otherwise, however well-told the story is, the children won't be able to transfer what they have learnt about God into their everyday lives.

Praying

In essence, prayer is talking to God as you would to a friend. The group leader's role is to dispel some of the mystery and embarrassment surrounding prayer, and to help the children grow in confidence. You can do this by using a variety of methods, and by being accepting of the children's efforts.

Prayers don't always have to be said out loud. They can be written down, drawn, sung or even just thought. Even when prayers are spoken, they could be the same thing said by everyone at once, different things said by everyone at once, individual prayers said one at a time, or in the form of a liturgy read by a leader with a corporate response.

By helping children to understand that prayer can be fun – that it is not just a matter of assuming the right pose and saying the right words in the right order – we are setting them free to enter a natural relationship with God, to talk to him about anything, anytime, anywhere.

Quizzes

Quizzes are a useful, enjoyable way of reinforcing the teaching point for the day. If the children are told there will be a quiz, they often pay closer attention to the story. By having a quiz, you can check that the main facts and significance of the story have been understood, and can correct misunderstandings without labouring the point too strongly. A quiz can be used at the beginning of a session to revise the teaching from a previous session.

Children love the competitive element of quizzes, but you need to watch that things don't get too aggressive. Random scoring methods are one way of keeping a quiz under control – they take away some of the pressure for every child to get every question right. The quiz-master will need to be scrupulously fair, as the children's strong sense of justice will rise to the surface if they feel their team is being hard done by. Choose your questions carefully, taking into account their ability levels. Keep it simple enough to involve all of them, not just the clever or knowledgeable ones.

Vary your approach week by week. You can use several different types of quiz questions – true or false, multiple choice, 'What/Who am I?', 'Unjumble the letters', 'Fill in the missing word', or 'Spot the deliberate mistake'. Create a scoring system that links into your teaching point for that week: for instance, if you were having a quiz on the story of Joseph, you may like to cut coat outlines out of card, write a different number on the back of each and peg them to a piece of string, like a washing line. When a child answers a question correctly they choose a coat and score, for their team, the number written on the back of it. If your story is about a banquet, feast, party or meal, set out paper cups on a table and allow the children to throw a foam ball at them; they score a point for each cup they knock down.

A quiz should be fast moving and over within five minutes. If it goes on too long, the children will become bored. Five or six questions for each side is usually ample.

Memory verses

Although we may long to see immediate spiritual fruit in the lives of the children who come to our clubs, the reality is that for many this is just a brief encounter with God on their journey through life. For that reason it is important that we take the opportunity to give them something that will remain with them after they have moved on. The psalmist writes, 'I have hidden your word in my heart that I might not sin against you' (Psalm 119:11, *NIV*). By encouraging children to learn memory verses, we are helping them to 'hide God's word in their hearts'.

Choose a verse that is relevant both to the topic of the day and to the children's own lives. Check that the meaning of the verse in its original context is the same as the meaning you are drawing out to illustrate your teaching point. Be sure that the children understand the words and the sense of the verse: for example, in the verse quoted above from Psalm 119, the language is simple enough but the sense may be confusing for infant children who use language literally. Look at different translations and choose the one that is the simplest and clearest. Stress the meaning of the verse rather than just the memorising of it. Include the biblical reference, even saying it twice, at the beginning and at the end, so that if the children do return to the verse in later years they have some clue as to where it came from. Link the verse into the teaching, and discuss with the children why it is relevant.

Learning memory verses should be lively, fun and fast moving. Provide visual cues, to start the children off. Here are some examples:

- Write each word of the verse on a separate balloon, and pop one every time the verse is repeated.
- Write the verse on rice paper and get the children to eat it.
- Do the verse as a jigsaw, gradually removing the pieces as they learn it.
- Write the verse onto a sheet of wrapping paper, fold it up and tear a corner off after every repetition.

Aim to repeat the words at least ten times, but vary the way they are said. They could be whispered, shouted, sung to the tune of 'Three blind mice', made into a rap, chanted while marching, or passed on as a Chinese Whisper. Revise the verses you learn regularly. Offer a prize at the end of term for anyone who can remember all that term's verses.

Music

Young children love to sing, although by the time they reach the top end of the primary school they may feel more self-conscious about doing so. Music is a very useful medium for getting teaching points across in a memorable way. Often we find ourselves still humming a song long after the event where we learnt it.

When choosing music, go for tunes that are lively and simple. Songs with actions are often popular, but don't discard quieter and more meditative ones. After talking about what Jesus has done for us, a song like 'I'm special' can allow children to make a thoughtful response. Remember that very lively music will hype the children up, but quieter songs will calm them down. It may be wise to have loud action songs at the beginning of the session and quieter songs at the end.

Look carefully at the language of the songs

you choose. Archaic words and religious vocabulary, which the children are likely to have had little exposure to, are probably not suitable for use in a school group. If there are only one or two difficult words and you decide to use the song, explain their meaning before asking children to sing. Be wary of songs with 'confessional' words such as 'I want to worship the Lord' or 'I love you, Lord Jesus' – songs that put into a singer's mouth words that may not be true. There is a place for using these songs as a response to God, but the leader needs to give the children a choice, perhaps saying something like, 'Read through the words and then only sing them if you really mean them.'

Games

People who lead clubs that take place straight after school often find that games are an important part of their programme. Children who have been sitting in lessons all day will have a lot of energy to expend. They need a chance to run around before they will be willing to sit down and listen. People who lead clubs that take place during a lunch-time may hardly ever include a game in their programme – time is very tight and the playground areas are full of other schoolchildren. The venue of the group and the number of children attending will also affect whether or not the leader decides to include games and, if so, what sort.

Apart from their enjoyment value, games also involve interaction and thus help to build up relationships within the group and to develop skills of cooperation. They encourage a sense of fair play and demonstrate the need for rules in order to achieve this. Games may be used just for fun as ice-breakers, but they can also introduce or illustrate a teaching point.

When choosing games, you will need to consider the following points.

Space
Is this a safe place to play this sort of game? Should it take place indoors or out?

The participants
Is this game suitable for their age and level of maturity? Will it help them let off steam?

Equipment
What will you need? Is it available?

Your own personality
Only lead games that you are comfortable with. Be prepared and know the game well.

Instructions
Avoid games that are too complicated. Give the instructions clearly and simply, insisting on quiet as you explain. Check that the participants have understood before you start the game.

Team selection
Don't allow team leaders to pick sides – this leads to children feeling inadequate and rejected if they are not picked straightaway. Find an arbitrary way of making teams, for example January-June birthdays versus July-December birthdays, with free transfers (decided by the leader) if numbers are not equal.

And, finally, choose games that all children can take part in, not just ones that favour the more athletic among them.

7

BROADENING THE OUTLOOK

The Christian group in a school will obviously be a witness to the children who attend. However, earlier on we touched on how the group could be a witness to the whole school or even to the wider community. It's time to explore this further.

Doing things in school

Most schools would probably be very grateful if your group offered to take an assembly once a term or once a year. The children may already take part in class assemblies fairly regularly, so the idea would not be a new one to them. However, the leader will need to bear in mind that there is far less practice-time available to a voluntary group meeting once a week than to a regular class. It's probably best to aim for something simple. For example, getting the children to mime while a Bible story is read is likely to be more successful than a drama that requires them to learn lines.

If the assembly follows the group's theme for the term, there may be a song they have sung over the term, which they could teach to the rest of the school. Or there may already be a song in the school's repertoire to fit the theme of the assembly.

There is plenty of scope for voluntary activities that will quietly make an impression. The children could pick up litter in the playground, do some weeding or make a cake for the staff. It's probably better to look for short-term, one-off activities than to take on a long-term responsibility. If the children's enthusiasm wanes, it will be left to the leaders to keep things going. Otherwise, it will seem to the school that the Christian group has not fulfilled its responsibilities.

You may feel it would be good to put on occasional events for the families of children in the club – a walk and picnic, a barbecue, a barn dance, a visit to the local swimming pool, or an 'It's a Knockout' type event could all work well. Getting to know the parents in an informal setting will help calm any fears they may have about what the leaders are trying to achieve and give the leaders a useful insight into the children's backgrounds.

If there are two or more school groups in an area, it may be possible to organise an inter-school event. This could be a fun day, an outing together, a quiz or a game of rounders. It will be encouraging for the children to meet with others of similar interests, and for the leaders to compare notes and realise they are not alone. If there is a Christian group in the local secondary school it would be good, towards the end of the academic year, to invite the leaders and some of the group members to come and meet children who will be moving up to that school. This will help bridge the gap and ensure that children from non-Christian homes continue to receive Christian teaching.

Doing things in the community

Helping the children to see what they could do in their local communities will encourage them to be 'givers' and not just 'takers'. What they can be involved in will depend on the sorts of opportunities for service the community provides. It might be carol singing at a home for the elderly at Christmas; making sandwiches for churches to distribute among the homeless; or devising a children's page, with puzzles, stories, pictures and jokes, for a community newspaper.

The wider world

There are a number of projects school groups can get involved in which will help the children understand more about world mission. Operation Christmas Child and Eurovangelism both organise the collection of gifts in shoeboxes for children who are refugees, usually in Eastern Europe. The group could set up a pen-pal partnership with a missionary, or with children of a similar age at a mission school in the two-thirds world. Alternatively, they could raise money for a particular mission or project by having a sale or some sort of sponsored event.

A few years ago *On Track* organised a project to raise money towards producing Bible-reading notes for children in Slovakia. All sorts of fund-raising activities took place. A JAFFA club ran a

Jaffa stall, selling Jaffa cakes and oranges. Another group were sponsored to read as much of Mark's Gospel as possible in a quarter of an hour. Sweets and cakes were made and sold at playtime. Yet another group spent one session of their club-time doing Bible puzzles in silence. The children in another club were sponsored to read a passage from their Bibles every day for a week. On average, each group raised about £10, which might not seem like a lot taken individually; but altogether £500 was raised – a significant proportion of the money needed.

8

POTENTIAL PROBLEMS

Most groups I have visited as a Scripture Union schools worker have one or two children who create problems every week. Some groups are full of those sort of children! It is hard to see why they attend, since they are disruptive, spoil the fun of the activities for others and get into trouble with the group leader all the time. It would be nice to suppose that they sense something of God's love in the way they are treated at the group, but perhaps they have just been banned from all other school clubs because of their behaviour. In reality, the leaders are usually praying they won't turn up so that they can have a break for just one week!

The children are not the only ones who create problems: they can arise in dealings with the school, with parents or within the leadership team. It is inevitable that when human beings are working together there will be problems, but they always seem to take us by surprise.

This chapter tells how some real-life problems were handled. You may have come across some of these already and have dealt with them very differently (after all, there is no one right way), or you may be trying to cope with similar situations at present. If so, perhaps these stories will help you think through the issues and give you more confidence in handling the downs as well as the ups of running your group.

Attention seeking

Carly, who is 8, started to repeat everything the leader said. It was exasperating. When she was asked to be quiet, Carly remarked that it was not her who was talking, it was 'Polly Parrot'. Eventually, the leader had had enough and asked Polly Parrot to leave. Carly got up, walked out of the room and disappeared.

If this had happened during a lunch-time group, the leader could just have let Carly go – she had been looking for attention in an inappropriate way. Chasing after her would have rewarded her bad behaviour. However, it happened after school when the leader was legally responsible for Carly. She could not even be sure that Carly had stayed on school premises. There was no other adult involved in running the club, so the leader sent a child to see if Carly was getting up to mischief outside and to make sure she didn't go home. The leader sent another child to find another adult – a teacher working in a classroom, or a cleaner – to ask if he or she would deal with Carly while she carried on running the club.

While Carly was out, the leader had a chat with the rest of the children. She asked them not to laugh at Carly or get annoyed with her when she was playing 'Polly Parrot', but to be friendly with her when she was behaving well.

After the club, the leader spoke to Carly to try to get to the bottom of her behaviour. Later she went to see Carly's class-teacher to find out whether there were problems with her in class and, if so, how the teacher dealt with them.

Spiritual questions

Jill had been praying for a while that she would see some spiritual fruit from her work among the children. However, she was really taken aback when, out of the blue, in the middle of trying to organise a craft activity with children clamouring for scissors, glue and pens, Hannah suddenly asked, 'Am I a Christian? How can I be one?' Jill had regarded the session as being divided up into time to talk about 'spiritual' things and time to do 'ordinary' things; but she realised that the children did not see the same distinctions.

Jill settled the children, then sat down beside Hannah to try to answer her question while she carried on making what she was making. She did not feel she should take Hannah away to speak to her privately, for a number of reasons:

- Hannah would miss the craft session, which might have a negative impact on her interest in spiritual things.
- She had asked her question publicly without embarrassment, and would probably find it

strange to be talked to in private, making it such an intense topic.

- Children often chat less self-consciously while their hands are busy.

- Other children might be interested in the same question. Talking to Hannah with the rest of the group around meant they could all hear Jill's answer.

- Jill wanted to avoid being in a situation where she was alone with a child, out of sight of anyone else.

First, Jill tried to find out what was behind Hannah's question and what her understanding of being a Christian was. She then explained how to become a Christian and left Hannah to make her own response. After the group-time, Jill made a point of contacting Hannah's parents to tell them about this incident and to explain what she had told Hannah.

Constant disruption

Michelle hit the group like a bombshell. On a typical week, she would rush in as soon as she was released from class, pick up a leader's guitar and drop it on the floor, punch another child and, when a leader tried to mediate, storm off into the corner to sulk. She would interrupt at the most crucial time in the teaching session, then tear up someone else's craft work for no reason at all. As the leaders tried to clear up after the group, she would pick up somebody's car keys and dance off with them. It was the same, week after week after week!

The leaders discussed banning Michelle from the group. However, they knew she would not hear about God from anyone else. It was obvious she was a disturbed little girl, and though banning her would help the group it would not help Michelle in the long run. The leaders talked to the head and to Michelle's class-teacher, to find out what strategies they were employing to deal with Michelle.

One positive thing the leaders decided they could do was to get Michelle a little notebook and offer to give her a sticker every time she completed an activity without being too disruptive. This gave her three or four opportunities each group-time to be rewarded, or to start again if she had been naughty.

The leaders allocated one person each week to give Michelle one-to-one attention, to sit next to her, stay alongside her and play games with her. They also found someone who would pray regularly specifically for her. In all their dealings, the leaders tried to stress that it was her behaviour that they did not like, not Michelle herself.

After much discussion, the leaders felt that if, when they had tried all they could, Michelle's behaviour did not improve, they might impose a temporary ban. They would warn her that if she behaved in a certain way she would not be allowed to come to the group the next week. There would only be one warning, no second or third chances, and if she did misbehave the ban would be imposed. The leaders felt that if Michelle really did want to come to the group, she would make an effort to fulfil her side of the deal once she saw that they really meant what they said. (Even if she didn't, they felt that a week's respite without Michelle would do them and the other children some good!)

Progress was slow but, over the course of a year and a half, Michelle did gradually improve.

Dealing with differences

The group seemed to have become very polarised. Becky and Emma, both aged 11 and in Year 6, had been coming to the group for more than three years; all the other children were aged 7–8 and in Years 3 or 4. Becky and Emma were Christians from Christian homes; none of the others had any church contact at all. Becky and Emma began to get very impatient with the newcomers, who were, in their opinion, spoiling the group.

Mary, the group leader, spoke privately to Becky and Emma. She suggested that since the two girls were getting a lot of spiritual input both at home and at church, perhaps they ought to see the school group as an opportunity to serve God and to help the younger children come to know more about him. She gave them responsibilities: each week they served out squash and biscuits, washed up the cups and prayed for the group. Occasionally Mary also asked them to lead a quiz, share a testimony or work alongside some of the less able children.

Over the course of the year, Becky and Emma became a valuable resource to Mary, and they were helped towards spiritual maturity themselves.

Inappropriate help?

Barbara was running the group on her own and was desperate for help. When Danielle's mum, Pat, offered to come along, Barbara was quick to accept. Then she discovered that Pat was not married to Danielle's father, although they were in a long-term relationship and had three children of school-age. Barbara also learned that Pat had started attending a local spiritualist church.

Although she wished she had taken the time to find out more beforehand, Barbara felt that having accepted Pat's offer of help she could not now decide to reject it. She felt that Pat was looking for truth and meaning in her life – which was why she had joined the spiritualists and why she had offered to help Barbara. Barbara made a commitment to pray for Pat regularly.

There were plenty of practical things Barbara could ask Pat to do without getting her involved with the spiritual teaching – serving squash and biscuits, working alongside the children at craft and supervising games. Barbara chatted to Pat, explaining the aims of the group and her personal reasons for running it.

Pat helped very willingly for about a year. Then, when Danielle left the group, she did too. God only knows what effect that time will have had on her life, but Barbara makes sure that she no longer assumes that all offers of help come from Christians.

Above reproach

Matt was a young man in his twenties, who had come to help run the group at school. The children, mostly girls, loved him. They fought to sit next to him; they wanted him to give them piggybacks; they clung on to him at every opportunity. Matt did not seem to see this as a problem, but some of the other leaders felt a little uneasy about the situation.

It was decided, after some discussion, that Matt should be made gently aware that unnecessary physical contact with the children should be avoided. In today's society, perfectly innocent actions could easily be misinterpreted.

The leaders worked together to help diffuse the situation. They divided the children into groups for some activities, giving a leader responsibility for each group. Matt had a group of boys, and sometimes he would adjudicate rather than join in the games. Once he was aware of the dangers of the situation, he made great efforts to prevent the girls from monopolising him.

Avoiding misunderstandings

The head told Margaret that the group would have to close. He had had several complaints from parents that she was indoctrinating the children.

Margaret's first reaction was shock. She had been telling the children how people could become Jesus' friends and live God's way, and she had offered them the chance to become Jesus' friends themselves. However, there was certainly no indoctrination. She prayed God would give her wisdom to handle the situation.

Margaret then spent time evaluating what she had done which might have caused offence. Had she used figurative language that the children had taken literally and misunderstood? Had she made it clear that becoming a Christian was *their* choice, and let them make up their own minds? Was what she did appropriate for the children's stage of intellectual, emotional and spiritual development? Had she been responsible in her approach?

Margaret contacted a local Scripture Union schools worker to talk through these issues and to hear an objective opinion. However, having considered everything, she was fairly sure she had acted rightly in her dealings with the children.

Margaret made an appointment to see the head. She asked him whether he knew specifically what the parents were upset about. She explained what she had been trying to achieve, showed him the resource booklet she had been using, and invited him to visit the group to see for himself. (He did not actually take up the invitation.)

Margaret invited the parents to a meeting so that they could explain their misgivings. She would also have the opportunity to explain directly to them what she had been trying to do and, if necessary, apologise for any misunderstanding. When one particular parent got quite vocal, Margaret reminded everyone that the group was voluntary and they could withdraw their children if they were unhappy. A group of Christian parents were very helpful as mediators, outlining what they felt were the benefits of the group.

The group was allowed to continue. Margaret made a point at the start of each term of showing the head the programme she would be using, so that he had the opportunity to raise any objections beforehand. The Christians who had acted as mediators made a commitment to pray regularly for the group. None of the children were withdrawn by their parents.

Dwindling interest

A group that had been running successfully for five years suddenly seemed to drop in numbers. For several weeks there were only four or five children, then one week there was only one. The following week nobody came. The group leader discovered that over the years, although the group was open to all the children in the junior section of the school, it had got a reputation for being only for girls and lower junior children. Now a dance club had started on the same afternoon for lower-junior girls, and most of the former members of the Christian group had gone to join that.

It seemed to the leader that there were two options. One was to stop running the group completely; the other was to close it for a term and then relaunch it on a different afternoon with a different name. After discussion with the head, the leader decided to go for the second option.

While the group was temporarily closed the leader updated herself on resources and ideas, visiting one or two other groups locally, to broaden her outlook. This meant that when the group restarted, she was fresh and enthusiastic. The new name seemed to catch the children's imagination, and several boys as well as girls came along. The group is once again running successfully.

9

PROGRAMME OUTLINES

This section contains ideas for group programmes based on six different themes. All these resources were previously printed in *On Track*, Scripture Union's termly booklet for people running Christian groups in schools.

NB The songs listed can be found in *Junior Praise*, the combined words edition.

WHAT'S GOD LIKE?

HE LIKES MAKING THINGS

Bible base
Genesis 1:1 – 2:4.

Teaching point
God likes to make things. He is creative, and our creativity is a reflection of his.

Introduction
Set up a craft activity where, using the same basic equipment, the children can make a variety of things, as follows:

- Decorating biscuits using butter-icing, icing pens, hundreds and thousands, chocolate chips, etc.
- Modelling balloons into different shapes.
- Making fridge magnets or badges from *Fymo* or salt dough. To make salt dough, mix flour, salt and hot water in the ratio 4:1:1. Then, when the dough has been modelled, bake it for two hours in the oven at 150°C.

Link
Look at the variety of things the children have made. Point out how different each of the items is, even though they were all made from the same material. Ask the children if they enjoyed the activity. Tell them that when we have fun making things and creating variety, we are being like God.

Main input
Tell the story of creation (Gen 1:1 – 2:4). If you can get hold of cheap white T-shirts, you could draw on them with fabric pens to represent each day's creation, then get the children to model them as you tell the story. Alternatively, draw with a candle onto white sheets of paper, then brush over your drawing with watery paint as you tell the story.

- *In the Beginning* by Stephanie Jeffs (a Tamarind book, available from Scripture Union) emphasises the vast variety in creation and God's pleasure in all he has made.

Application
Discuss with the children which colour they would miss most if all the world was only black and white. What would it be like if God had only made one type of animal, tree, flower, fruit or vegetable? Do we really need variety, or is it just a bonus from God?

Response
- *Sing:* 'He made the water wet' (JP 359).
- Cut out flower-petal shapes and write prayers on them, thanking God for the things he has made. Then make flowers out of them and put the flowers all together to make a bouquet.

HE IS TRUSTWORTHY

Bible base
Genesis 6:9 – 9:17.

Teaching point
God always tells the truth and keeps his promises, so we can trust him.

Introduction
Ask the children to find a partner. One of the pair is then blindfolded and led round the room by his or her partner. Older children may enjoy having obstacles to go around, under or over. After they have played the game for a while, ask the partners to change roles.

Link
Ask the children whether they found it easy to trust the other person while they themselves were unable to see where they were going. Talk about trust, and find out the kind of people they trust and why.

Main input
Tell the story of Noah (Gen 6:9 – 9:17) using a prop box. Put the following items into the box:

name-labels for the eight people on the ark
toy tools
bits of wood
plastic animals
umbrellas
cagoules
sunglasses
a picture of a rainbow

Ask eight children to help you. Tell the story, taking the appropriate items out of the prop box for your helpers to hold up. Alternatively, tell the story while they do the sound effects (eg sawing, hammering, laughter, animal noises, rain).

Application
Ask the children whether they thought it was easy or difficult for Noah to trust God when everyone else was laughing at him. Noah trusted God to look after him, his family and the animals as he had promised, and God kept his promise. At the end of the story God made another promise – that he would never again destroy the world with a flood – and he is still keeping that promise. Ask the children if they can think of any more of God's promises.

Response
- *Sing:* 'Mister Noah built an ark' (JP 167).

- Talk together about the last chorus of the song. When we see a rainbow, it reminds us that God loves us and we can trust him fully.

- Here are some of the things God has promised us:

  'I will always be with you, I will never leave you.'
  'Whatever you do, I will love you.'
  'If you say sorry for the wrong things you have done, I will forgive you.'
  'When you pray, I will listen and answer.'

- Let the children choose their favourite promise to copy out onto a piece of A5 card and decorate. Punch two holes into the top of the card and attach some string, to make a wall-hanging. Encourage the children to hang the promises where they will see it and remember that God keeps his promises to us.

- Collect large boxes from a local supermarket, and make a model of the ark.

HE KNOWS EVERYTHING

Bible base
Genesis 40:1 – 41:36.

Teaching point
God knows everything, including what will happen in the future.

Introduction
Play a general knowledge quiz, eg Blockbusters.

Link
Point out to the children that some of them obviously know quite a lot about certain subjects, but only God knows everything about everything.

Main input
You could either show episode 2 of the video *Joseph* (Scripture Union), or tell the story of Joseph (Gen 40:1 – 41:36) using clues. Before the start of the session, hide numbered envelopes around the room, each containing one of the following items:

Envelope no. 1: a pair of toy handcuffs
Envelope no. 2: a bread roll and some grapes
Envelope no. 3: a sticker saying 'Don't forget'
Envelope no. 4: a plastic cow
Envelope no. 5: a gold chain and a ring

Invite the children to find the envelopes in turn, and then discuss together what part of the story the clues might be pointing to.

Application
Ask the children how Joseph was able to interpret the dreams. Draw out the point that only God knows what is going to happen. Sometimes people read their stars or tarot cards to try and find out the future, but these things are really a waste of time. God does not show the future through them; in fact he warns us not to meddle with them. He is the only one who really knows everything.

Response
- *Memory Verse:* Learn Jeremiah 29:11. Write the words out on paper cow-shapes, and gradually remove each word as the children learn the verse.

  'I know the plans I have for you,'
  declares the Lord, 'plans to prosper you
  and not to harm you, plans to give you
  hope and a future.'

  Jeremiah 29:11, NIV

- *Sing:* 'My Lord is higher than a mountain' (JP 170).

HE IS POWERFUL

Bible base
Exodus 6:28 – 12:42.

Teaching point
God is far more powerful than the greatest human authority.

Introduction
Uncrown the King: Choose one child to be the king. Place a tall paper crown on his head and seat him at one side of the room, with his back to the others. The rest of the group stand at the far side of the room and throw screwed-up bits of newspaper to try and knock the crown off the king's head. When the king is 'uncrowned', a new king is chosen.

Link
Set the scene for the story, explaining that God's people, the Israelites, were slaves in Egypt under a powerful and cruel king known as Pharaoh. God chose Moses to be his special messenger to tell Pharaoh to let them go.

Main input
Tell the story of the plagues (Exod 6:28 – 12:42). You could either show episode 3 from the *Exodus* video (SU), or use the following rap (from *Learning All Together*, Oct–Dec 1991):

The Egyptian Rap

Keep the beat going by clicking fingers on every second beat.

Lord God sent Moses to Pharaoh one day
To ask that king to let his people go away,
Gave Aaron power with a special stick,
But Pharaoh said, 'Anyone can do that trick!'

Chorus

But Pharaoh said, 'No',
Yes, Pharaoh said, 'No',
Yes, Pharaoh said, 'No, no, no, no, no!'

Lord God changed the river from water to blood.
The frogs jumped out and they landed thud.
They came in the house, they jumped in the streets,
People found them in their beds and under their sheets.

Chorus

Then gnats and flies came buzzing around.
Every room was filled with a ghastly sound.
The people scratched and the people cried
When one day they heard that all the animals had died.

Chorus

Then boils popped up all over their skin –
Didn't matter if they were fat or thin.
The hail beat down and the locusts came,
But still old Pharaoh said just the same.

Chorus

Then God sent darkness all over the land –
You couldn't see the sky and you couldn't see your hand.
An angel came down and the first-born died.
All over the land, the Egyptians cried.

Then Pharaoh said, 'Go',
Yes, Pharaoh said, 'Go',
Yes, Pharaoh said, 'Go, go, go, go, go!'

Application
Ask the children why they think God sent the plagues, and why Pharaoh was so stubborn. Discuss together what this story shows us about God's power.

Response
- *Sing:* 'What a mighty God we serve' (JP 491), 'My Lord is higher than a mountain' (JP 170).
- *Memory Verse:* Learn Daniel 6:26, using the maze opposite.

  'He is the living God, the one who lives for ever. His power and his kingdom will never end.'

  Daniel 6:26

What's God like?

Follow the maze to discover the verse.

HE IS LOVING

Bible base
Luke 15:1–7.

Teaching point
God loves everyone, whatever they are like.

Introduction
Hunt the Thimble: Use a model or picture of a sheep instead a thimble. Ask the children to make a loud 'Baa-ing' sound if the searcher is near the sheep, and to go quieter when she moves farther away.

Link
Make the point that the sheep was very important to the searcher. Ask the searchers how they felt when they actually found the sheep. Have any of the children ever lost anything and had to search for it? Have any of them been lost themselves?

Main input
Tell the story of the lost sheep (Luke 15:1–7). If you can, get hold of a sheep-puppet and tell the story from the lost sheep's point of view. Express amazement that the shepherd cared enough to keep looking until the sheep was found.

Application
Discuss with the children what they would have done if they had been the shepherd. Point out the meaning of the story, which is that everyone, no matter who they are or what they are like, is loved by God. Brainstorm together ways in which God shows his love to us.

Response
- *Sing:* 'Everyone in the whole wide world' (JP 333).

- *Sheep Badges:* Make a sheep shape with a pipe cleaner. Then wind wool around both the pipe cleaner and the top half of an open safety pin.

- There is a funsheet on this theme in *Theme Fun* by Lesley and Neil Pinchbeck (now out of print, but some bookshops may still have copies). And *Let's Explore Inside the Bible* by Fiona Walton (available from Scripture Union) has some additional craft ideas to do with sheep.

HE IS FAIR

Bible base
Matthew 18:21–35.

Teaching point
God is fair, and he wants us to show justice and fairness to others.

Introduction
Divide the children into three teams to play a game, Snakes and Ladders. Each team plays under different rules: Team 1 has to shake the dice to move, so all their moves are decided at random; Team 2 can choose any number they like between 1 and 6, therefore they play strategically, taking advantage of the ladders and avoiding the snakes; and Team 3 can only move 4 spaces (no more, no less) each time, regardless of the snakes or ladders they encounter along the way.

Link
Ask the children whether they thought the game was fair and how they felt about it. Brainstorm situations where they have heard or said the phrase 'It's not fair'. Discuss what they do when they experience unfairness. Do they tell anyone? How do they sort it out?

Main input
- Tell the story of the unforgiving servant (Matt 18:21–35). Older children could look the story up in the Bible and act it out in small groups. Younger children would be better acting out the story as you tell it.
- Divide the children into two teams and hold a quiz on the story. Whenever a team gets a question right, give them a piece of a jigsaw with one word from Psalm 103:6 written on it.

  For all who are ill-treated, the Lord
  brings justice.

  Psalm 103:6

Application
Tell the children that the Bible verse on their jigsaw shows how concerned God is about unfairness. He is often on the side of those who are treated unfairly, just like the king in the story was. Ask the children how God might want us to treat others. Bring out the point that God expects us to treat all others in a fair manner, and to look out for the needs of everyone, not just ourselves and our best friends. Look back at the unfair situations that were discussed earlier. Ask the children how they could show fairness in them.

Response
- Form a rugby tackle and pray about unfair situations, asking for God's help to show fairness to others.
- End by giving out some food, eg a packet of crisps or sweets, to be shared fairly among those present.

HE DOESN'T CHANGE

Bible base
Malachi 3:6a.

Teaching point
Whatever else changes in the world around us, God doesn't change.

Introduction
Musical Statues: The children dance around to music and, whenever the music stops, they freeze to form a statue. Anyone who moves is given one of the following letters – C, H, A, N, G, E. Stop the game as soon as a child has received enough letters to spell out the full word – 'CHANGE'.

Link
Ask the children what word was spelt by the letters in the game they have just played. Then divide them into groups, and each group brainstorms together to come up with a list of things that change. See who can come up with the longest list in three minutes. Ask if anyone has thought of anything that never ever changes.

Main input
Write out Malachi 3:6a – 'I am the Lord, and I never change' – in block letters. Then gradually reveal the message by painting in the letters one at a time. Remind the children that because God does not change, everything we learn about him from the Bible is still true of him today, thousands of years later. God still likes making things, keeps his promises, knows everything, loves everyone. He is still powerful and fair. Whatever else changes in life, we can be certain that God will remain the same.

Application
Hold a quiz on the stories covered in this series 'What's God like?' to remind the children of the characteristics of God we have been looking at. In a time of quiet, ask the children to think which of these characteristics is most important to them at the moment.

Response
- Make cardboard spinners that appear to change colour as they are spun.
- Play with colour-change play-dough.
- On a roll of lining paper or wallpaper, use colour-change pens or crayons to make a graffiti wall about God and his characteristics.

WHAT A NOISE!

SINGING AND MUSIC

Bible base
Luke 2:8–20.

Teaching point
Jesus' birth is good news, worth celebrating and singing about.

Introduction
Musical Instruments: Depending on the age of the children and the time available, you could try making plastic-bottle shakers, cardboard trumpets, paper-plate tambourines, drums using greaseproof paper secured over yoghurt pots by elastic bands, guitars using plastic meat-trays and elastic bands, and so on.

Link
Make a list of the times the children hear music, make music or feel like singing.

Main input
Tell the story of the angels and the shepherds (Luke 2:8–20). You could use the video or storybook of *The Grumpy Shepherd* (SU), or get the children to tell you the story by asking them a series of questions.

Application
Discuss why the angels and the shepherds might have thought that Jesus' birth was something to sing about. Ask the children whether they think it is still good news today to know that Jesus was born all those years ago. Encourage them to give reasons for their answers.

Response
- Sing a Christmas carol that mentions the angels and the shepherds. Give everyone the opportunity to play the instruments they made during the first activity.
- *Paper-doily angels*: Fold a circular paper doily into quarters, to form the angel's body. Stick a small circle of paper over the pointed end, to form the head. Cut another doily into quarters, and stick two of these behind the body to make wings. Draw in the facial features. Stick a scrap of tinsel on the head, to be the halo.
- Write your own songs of praise.
- Finish either one of the following sentences in as many different ways as you can: 'Jesus' birth was good news for…'; 'Jesus' birth was good news because…'

MECHANICAL SOUNDS

Bible base
Luke 2:39–40; Matthew 13:55; Mark 6:3.

Teaching point
Jesus had a normal childhood, so he understands what it is like to be a child.

Introduction
Photocopy the sheet opposite onto different coloured pieces of paper, making twice as many copies as the number of children in your group. Cut half of the copies into individual pictures and hide them around the room. Give each child a sheet of pictures and a little ball of *Blu-tack*. They have to find the individual pictures that match and stick them onto their sheet.

Link
Talk about the pictures, asking questions like 'What might you use this tool for? What noise does that make? Have you ever used something like this?' Make sure you mention 'carpenter' and talk about what a carpenter does.

Main input
Talk together about family life in Bible times. *Let's Explore Inside the Bible* by Fiona Walton will give you background information about the schools, toys and education of the day. Jesus would have gone to lessons at the synagogue from the age of six, and would have learnt his father's trade, carpentry. Show some tools Joseph might have used, eg an axe, a saw, a mallet, a stone-headed hammer, a chisel, a file, a plane, a bow-drill and bits, an awl, nails, a ruler, dividers and chalk. Mention that children were not considered important and they did not have much choice about what they wanted to do in life.

Application
Ask the children what they think Jesus might have enjoyed as a child and what he might have found difficult. Talk about the things they enjoy or find difficult.

Response
- Do some junk modelling with off-cuts of wood.
- Write your own prayers thanking God for the enjoyable things in life, and tell him about the difficult things, asking for his help.
- Play some games that Jesus might have played, eg hopscotch, ball games (throwing and catching), bowling hoops.

What a noise!

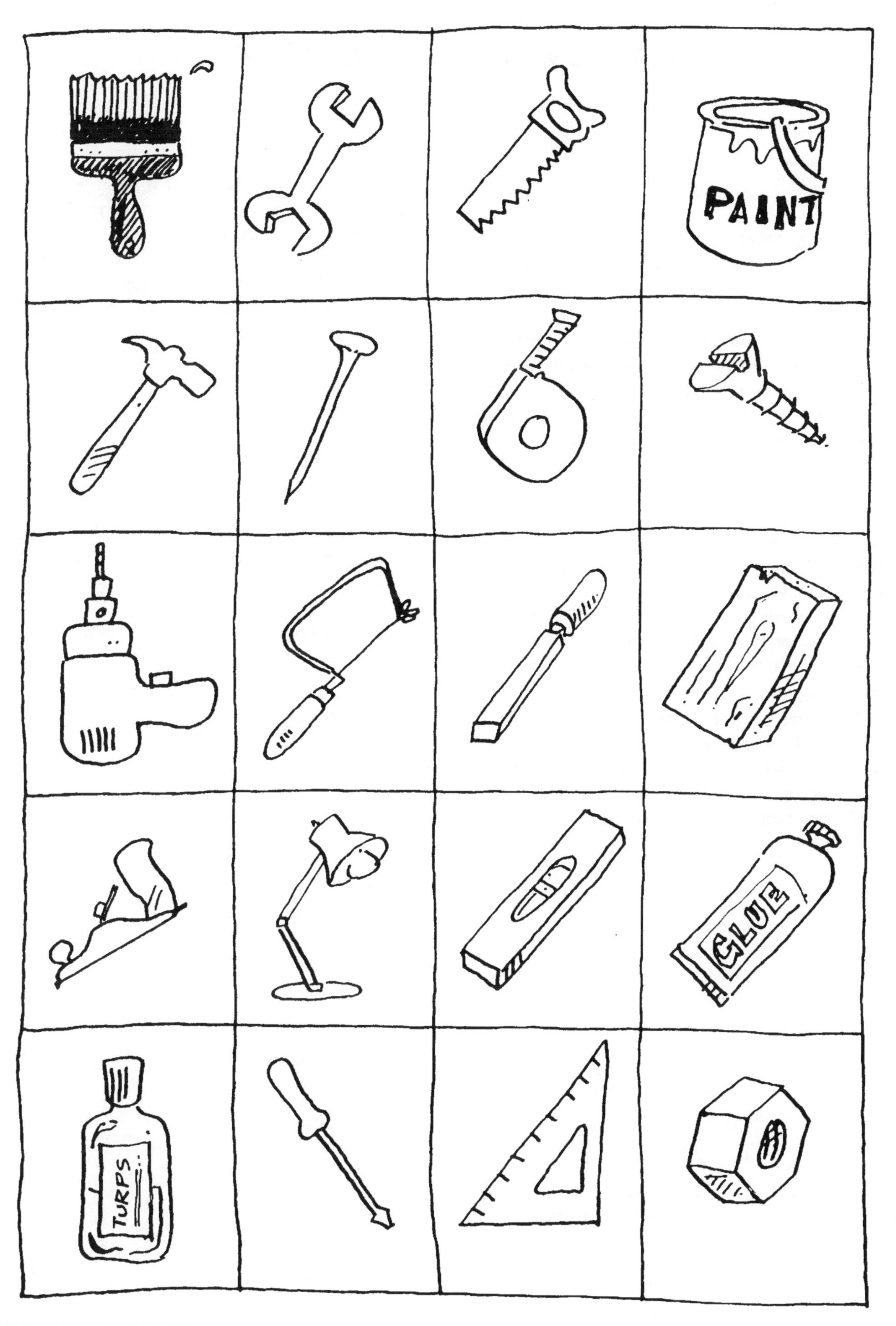

LAUGHTER AND CELEBRATION

Bible base
John 2:1–11.

Teaching point
We need to trust Jesus and do what he says.

Introduction
A Trust Game: In pairs, with one person blindfolded, the children guide each other through an obstacle course. Talk afterwards about how easy or difficult it was for the children to trust their partners to guide them while they were blindfolded.

Link
Start laying out party plates, cups, serviettes, and so on. Tell the children to put up their hands when they think they know what you are preparing for. Once it is established that you are preparing for a party, brainstorm together the different occasions for celebrating and having a party.

Main input
Tell the story of the wedding at Cana (John 2:1–11). Use the episode entitled 'The wedding' from the video *Signposts* (SU). Alternatively, make a story-cube, with each face of the cube showing a different scene from the story.

Application
Explain that this was the first miracle Jesus had ever done, so not even Mary would have known for sure what he could do to help. The servants would certainly have had no idea. Discuss what they might have felt like when Jesus told them to get all that water. What might they have felt like when he told them to take some 'water' to the man in charge? What might they have felt like when they realised all the water had turned into wine? Ask whether it was easy for them to trust Jesus. Talk about situations in which the children might find it easy or difficult to trust Jesus.

Response
- *Memory Verse:* Learn Psalm 37:5. Write each word on a paper cup, mix the cups up and ask the children put them in the right order.

  Let the Lord lead you and trust him to help.

  Psalm 37:5

- *Sing:* 'Give thanks to the Lord' (JP 345).

NATURAL SOUNDS

Bible base
Mark 4:35–41.

Teaching point
Jesus is powerful. We can trust him to help us.

Introduction
Play parachute games. If you do not have a parachute, or if your group is too small, use a large sheet or blanket instead.

Link
For your final parachute game, create a storm. Start with gentle waves and gradually build these up, making them more and more choppy. Tell the children that today's story is about a storm.

Main input
Tell the story of the calming of the storm (Mark 4:35–41). Divide the children into groups and give each group a sound effect to make at the appropriate time in the story, eg wind, waves, thunder, boat creaking, disciples shouting. Practise getting louder and louder, but then stopping instantly when you give the signal. Tell the story, bringing each sound effect in at the appropriate time, like a conductor.

Application
Discuss what the disciples learnt about Jesus from this incident. Talk about the sorts of things that make us feel frightened. Ask how Jesus can help us when we feel afraid.

Response
- Do the funsheet on p 46. Cut out the boat and colour the picture. Then attach the boat to the dot in the middle with a paper fastener, so that it can rock in the water.

- *Sing:* 'With Jesus in the boat' (JP 291).

THE BOAT IN THE STORM

SILENCE

Bible base
Mark 7:31–37.

Teaching point
Jesus has power over illness and physical disability. He can do amazing things.

Introduction
- *Dead Lions:* The children lie on the floor as still as they can. The leader moves among them, trying to provoke them into moving. Any child who moves is out. The winner is the last person still on the floor.

- Play Pictionary, stressing that there must be no verbal clues.

Link
Ask whether the children found it easy to be quiet and still (if you played Dead Lions) or not to talk at all (if you played Pictionary). Sometimes we like to be quiet, while at other times we enjoy making a lot of noise. Remind the children that some people have to live in silence all the time, like the person in the story.

Main input
Tell the story of the deaf-mute man (Mark 7:31–37). You could show the video from *Mark Time* (SU). Alternatively, get the children to act out the story as you tell it, choosing someone to be Jesus, someone to be the man and the rest to be the crowd.

Application
Ask the children what the man who was healed might have felt like. What might the crowd have thought? What would *they* have felt if they had been there? Discuss things about God that are amazing: he's so powerful, he loves us whatever we are like, and so on.

Response
Write 'The people were amazed at what Jesus did' in large block letters on A5 or A4 sheets of paper. Get the children to write or draw prayers of thanks inside each letter, and then to cut the letters out. Punch holes into the top corner of each letter and thread them onto a piece of string, making some prayer-bunting.

SHOUTING AND CHEERING

Bible base
Luke 19:28–38.

Teaching point
It is good to thank and praise God for the things he does for us.

Introduction
Divide the children into teams. Have a couple of fun relay races, eg the children could blow a feather, or hop. Encourage the teams to cheer and support their runners.

Link
Talk about events where people shout and cheer, eg football matches, a sports day, when somebody achieves something, when royalty or celebrities visit a place.

Main input
Tell the story of the ride into Jerusalem (Luke 19:28–38). You could give a show using shadow puppets projected on an OHP.

Application
Have a brainstorming session. What are the things the people might have known about Jesus which made them want to shout and cheer? What had he done for them? What had they heard him say? What difference had he made to their lives? Talk about the things we know about Jesus which we can thank and praise him for.

Response
- *Palm Branches:* Roll up a sheet of paper tightly and tape the edge. Make several cuts from the top to about a third of the way down. Gently pull the cut ends up from the centre.

- Make up some 'praise chants' to be sung or shouted, while waving the palm branches.

- Make a collage picture of the ride into Jerusalem.

CRYING

Bible base
Mark 15:1–41.

Teaching point
Because Jesus died, we can be friends with God.

Introduction
- If you have a group of older children, divide them into teams and give each team a copy of the same newspaper. Call out particular phrases taken from headlines, advertisements, and so on. The first person to bring you the relevant page from their newspaper earns a point for their team.

- Younger children can draw pictures of their friends. Then talk together about what makes someone a good friend.

Link
- Older children can look at their newspapers again to find items of bad news, eg violence, accidents, disasters, war. Brainstorm together the things that make people cry.

- With younger children, talk together about how sad we feel when friends won't share or play with us, when they fall out with us, when they go off on holiday or move away.

Main input
Tell the story of Jesus' death (Mark 15:1–41). You could use the following videos (all available from Scripture Union): the episode entitled 'The Crucifixion' from *Mark Time*; 'Good Friday' from *Good Friday/Easter Sunday*; or (with older children) 'The Champion' from *The Challenger & The Champion*. (Be sure to mention that his death was not the end – Jesus came back to life again. Next week's programme will be looking at that part of the story.)

Application
Ask the children why they think God let Jesus die. Explain that God punished Jesus instead of punishing people, and this made it possible for anyone to become his friend, if they say sorry and really mean it. It doesn't matter how bad we are, God will forgive us if we really mean our repentance.

Response
- *Memory Verse:* Learn Romans 5:10. Write it out in code for the children to work out.

  Even when we were God's enemies, he
  made peace with us, because his Son
  died for us.

  Romans 5:10

- On post-it notes, ask the children to write prayers telling Jesus what they think about his death. Stick the prayers on a large cross drawn in outline.

- *Sing:* 'I'm special' (JP 106).

TALKING

Bible base
Luke 24:13–35.

Teaching point
Whether we realise it or not, Jesus is always with us. We can always talk to him.

Introduction
Bring in photographs or pictures of well-known people or cartoon characters. Cover them with small pieces of paper attached with *Blu-tack*. Gradually remove the pieces of paper while the children try to guess as quickly as possible who is in the picture.

Link
Comment that to start with no one recognised the picture, but then suddenly it became obvious. Today's story is about two friends of Jesus who didn't recognise him at first.

Main input
Tell the story of the road to Emmaus (Luke 24:13–35). You could use an enlarged version of the story-wheel opposite, or show the episode entitled 'The Country House' from the video *Luke Street* (SU).

Application
Talk about the difference between what the friends were feeling at the beginning and at the end of the story. Why did Jesus' presence make such a difference? Point out that Jesus has promised he will always be with us. Ask the children at what times it would be especially important for them to remember that.

Response
- Make story-wheels of your own.

- *Sing:* 'Did you ever talk to God above?' (JP 329).

- On brick-shapes, ask the children to draw different situations they find themselves in (eg school, home, cubs, playground), or the times when they feel lonely or sad. Under each picture write 'Thank you, Jesus, that you are with me here'. Paste the brick-shapes onto a sheet of card inside the outline of a house. Then, at the top, write the words 'Jesus said, "I will be with you always" ' (Matt 28:20).

- Cut out the story-wheel.
- Draw around it on a plain piece of paper.
- Cut out the plain circle and then cut one segment from it.
- Fix the plain circle over the story-wheel, using a paper-fastener.
- Tell the story, showing one segment at a time!

THE ACTS OF THE HOLY SPIRIT

JESUS' ASCENSION

Bible base
Acts 1:6–11.

Teaching point
Even though Jesus was no longer going to be with his friends, he promised that the Holy Spirit would be with them (and us) always.

Introduction
- *Tramps Tea Party:* The children take turns to throw a dice. Whenever anyone throws a six, they put on a hat, scarf and gloves and, using a knife and fork, start to undo a bar of chocolate that has been wrapped up in several layers of newspaper. The next person to throw another six takes over, and the first person goes back to join the others in throwing the dice.

- Start telling a well-known story, eg Goldilocks and the Three Bears, then ask the children to continue.

- *Alphabet Stories:* In turn, the children contribute a sentence each as together they make up a story using successive letters of the alphabet.

Link
Point out that after Jesus had died, he came back to life again and appeared to his disciples. He spent time with them, but that time was limited and Jesus told them they must carry on. Ask the children to see if they can notice what the disciples are to carry on doing as you tell the story.

Main input
Tell the story of Jesus' ascension (Acts 1:6–11) using shadow puppets projected on an OHP.

Application
Discuss together how the children would feel if their best friend was leaving. What would they find helpful in that situation? Talk about how the disciples might have felt, drawing out the fact that when Jesus was around they had done amazing things. They may have been worried about how they would cope without him. But Jesus promised they would not be alone: the Holy Spirit would help them to carry on telling people about him.

Response
- *Memory Verse:* Learn Acts 1:8a. Write the words on an OHP acetate with a non-permanent pen, and rub them out as the children learn the verse.

  'The Holy Spirit will come upon you and
  give you power. Then you will tell
  everyone about me…'

  Acts 1:8

- *Sing:* 'Jesus, send me the helper' (JP 409).

PENTECOST

Bible base
Acts 2:1–14,38–42.

Teaching point
When the Holy Spirit came, he made a difference to people's lives.

Introduction
Fire and Wind Relays: The children could blow a paper cup along a length of string, play blow-football, or fan a flame-shaped piece of paper with a newspaper from one side of the room to the other.

Link
Discuss together what it is like waiting for something to happen. How do the children feel, waiting for a birthday, a school report?

Main input
Tell the story of Pentecost (Acts 2:1–14,38–42), drawing expressions on paper plates to show how the disciples felt at different stages. Alternatively, show the episode entitled 'Alight' from the video *On Fire!* (SU).

Application
Ask the children what effect the Holy Spirit had and who they think he is. Explain that the Holy Spirit is God, the invisible Helper. He is often described as a wind: you see the results of the wind, but can't actually see the wind itself; in the same way, you can see the results of friendship with God by the things God's friends do even though you can't see God himself. The Holy Spirit is God in action in the world.

Response
- Make newspaper headlines, covering the events of the story, or tape 'radio interviews' with eyewitnesses.

- *Flame Spinners:* You will need the spinner design opposite, stuck onto card; a length of string (approx 90 cm); a sharp point to make holes with; felt tips, glue and scissors. To make the spinners:

  Cut out the spinner designs and stick the two circles together.

  Colour in the flame shapes.

  The leader should make holes in the spinners. Then insert the string and knot the ends of the looped string together.

  Place the looped string over the forefinger of each hand. Twist the spinner around by holding one hand still and making circular movements with the other, so that the string becomes twisted. Then gently pull your hands apart and relax the string slightly.

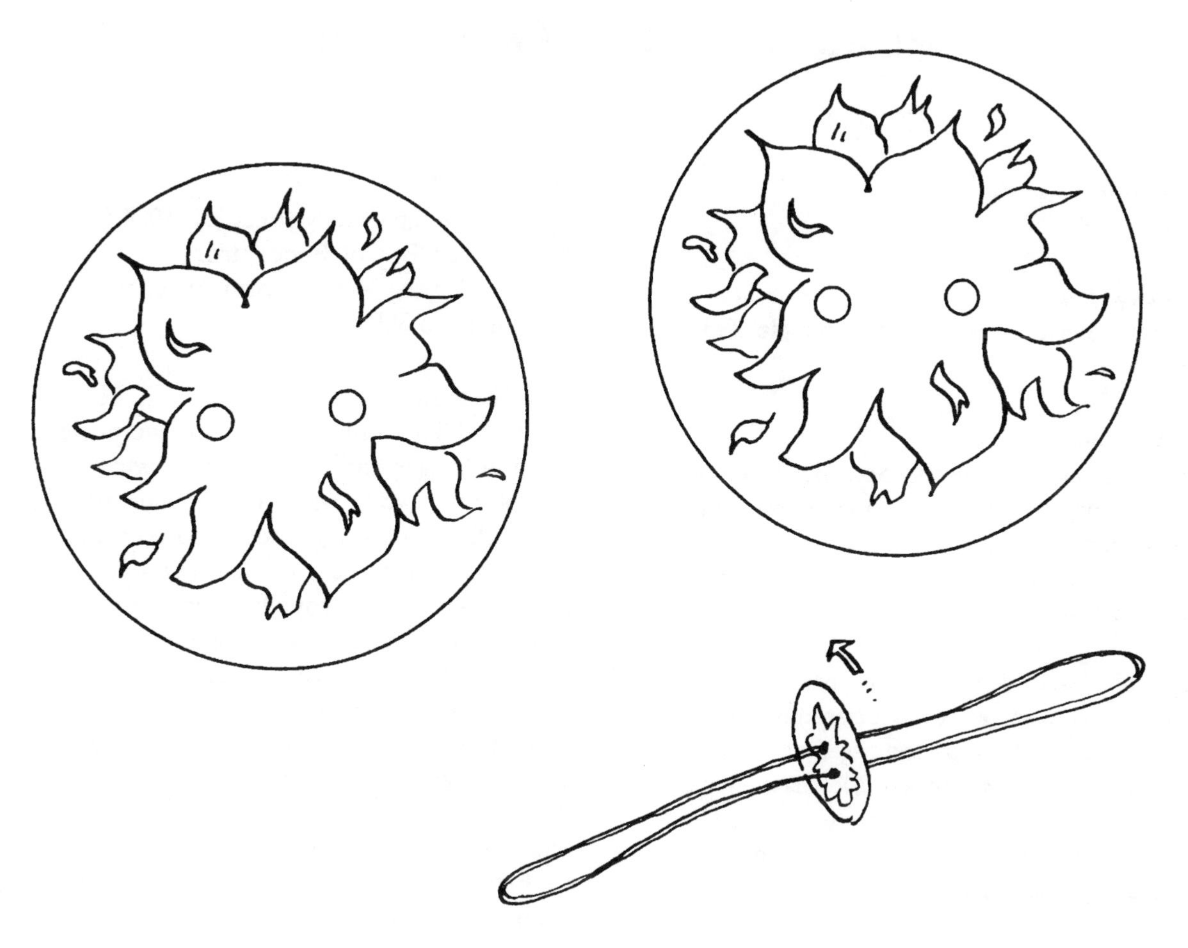

HEALING THE LAME MAN

Bible base
Acts 3:1–10; 4:1–21.

Teaching point
The Holy Spirit gives ordinary people God's power.

Introduction
- *Just a Minute:* (Or *Twenty Seconds*, depending on the age of your group members!) For a set time-limit, the children have to talk about a topic without hesitating or repeating themselves.

- *A Word-Association Game*: In pairs, children take turns to say words associated with those given them by their partner, eg shoe – leather – cow-hide – cow – milk... Alternatively, play Chinese Whispers, passing a message down a line of children, each one whispering it into the ear of the next.

Link
Point out that in today's story, the Holy Spirit helps Peter and John know what to say in a difficult situation.

Main input
Act out the Bible story (Acts 3:1–10; 4:1–21), or show either 'Bag of Bones' from the video *On Fire!*, or 'Making Waves' from *Shipshapes* (both available from SU).

Application
Ask the children where Peter got the power to heal the beggar and how he knew what to say. Demonstrate your point by showing them an empty glove and trying to tell it to do some simple things, eg pick up a book, carry a cup, touch somebody; then put your hand in the glove and repeat your commands, carrying them out as you do. Ask the children what made the difference. Just like the glove on its own is useless, Peter had been scared and powerless. But as a glove with a hand in it can do lots of things, Peter, when he was filled with the Holy Spirit, became bold and powerful. Refer back to the memory verse on page 53. Peter and John were doing what Jesus told them to do in that verse.

Response
Sing: 'Jesus, send me the helper' (JP 409), 'Be bold' (JP 14).

PHILIP AND THE ETHIOPIAN

Bible base
Acts 8:26–40.

Teaching point
The Holy Spirit helps us to understand what God is saying through the Bible.

Introduction
- Write out short messages in different codes on separate sheets of paper. Write out the code-breakers on other sheets of paper. Give the children one sheet each. Every child with a code needs to find another with the matching code-breaker. When they do, they can work out the message together.

- One child, or the leader, draws a picture and describes it to the others in the group to draw. Compare the finished results.

Link
Talk about things that are difficult to understand, eg maths, science. Give personal examples. The Holy Spirit provides someone to help the man in today's story to understand the Bible.

Main input
Tell the story of Philip and the Ethiopian (Acts 8:26–40), using wooden-spoon puppets. Alternatively, show the episode entitled 'The Riddle' from the video *On Fire!*

Application
The Bible isn't an easy book but it is important because it tells us more about Jesus. Ask the children if there are things about God and the Bible that they do not understand. Start a question box for them to put their questions in. If the questions are put in anonymously, answer them to the whole group. If a child signs her name on the question, give her a written answer. Advertise children's Bible-reading notes, such as *Let's Go* for 7–8s and *Check it Out!* for 9–11s.

Response
- *Memory Verse:* Learn Psalm 119:18. Write it out in code, or introduce it in a game of Hangman.

  Open my mind
  and let me discover the wonders of
  your Law.

  Psalm 119:18

- *Sing:* 'God loves you so much' (JP 349).

- *Pairs Tag:* Two children are 'It' and run around as a pair. When they catch someone, that person joins onto the catcher by holding him by the waist. When four children are joined together, they split into two pairs.

THE CONVERSION OF PAUL

Bible base
Acts 9:1–19.

Teaching point
The Holy Spirit changes people's lives and brings them to God.

Introduction
- Show the children a tray of assorted objects. Then take the tray away and remove one of the objects, or add another. Show the children the tray again and see if they can notice the difference.

- In pairs, the children stand facing their partners. One of the pair turns round and alters her appearance slightly, eg removes a hair-slide, loosens a tie. Then she turns back to face her partner once again. Her partner has to guess what has changed.

Link
Show the children objects, or pictures of objects, which they have to match up into pairs. Then talk about what has happened to make each object a little different from its partner, eg water/ice-cube, cake-mix/cake, seed/plant, dirty plate/clean plate.

Main input
Put the children into two groups, and read the story of Paul's conversion (Acts 9:1–19) while the groups mime it simultaneously. Alternatively, show the episode entitled 'Blinded' from the video *On Fire!*

Application
Discuss the ways in which Paul changed and what made the difference. Ask the children whether they think that the Holy Spirit can change people today.

Response
- Ask the children to think of some way they would like the Holy Spirit to help them change. Tell them to speak to the Holy Spirit in their minds, asking him to do what they have just thought of. The leader can bring the silence to a close by saying a prayer out loud.

- In teams, the children race to make a 'new man' by stuffing newspaper into old trousers and sweatshirt. (Fasten the ends of the arms and legs with elastic bands and use a balloon to make a head.)

PETER AND CORNELIUS

Bible base
Acts 10:1–48.

Teaching point
The Holy Spirit is available for everyone.

Introduction
- *Sheet Volleyball*: Divide the group into two teams, and group each team around a sheet. The teams then toss a ball from one sheet to the other.

- *Animal Pictionary:* Divide the children into teams. Each team sends a representative to the leader. The leader gives the representative the name of an animal which he has to then communicate to his team by drawing only – no talking is allowed. The first person in the team to guess which animal it is goes up to the leader as the next representative. The winning team is the first one to guess all the animals on the leader's list; or to guess the most animals within a pre-set time-limit.

Link
Sing: 'Jesus, send me the helper' (JP 409), 'Sing praise to God the Father' (JP 455).

Main input
Tell the story of Peter and Cornelius (Acts 10:1–48), using a box containing some appropriate props, eg a sheet, plastic animals, an angel, a flat-roofed house. Explain clearly beforehand that Jewish law forbids the eating of certain foods (these are listed in Deuteronomy 14:3–21).

Application
Emphasise that up to this time the good news about Jesus had only been passed on to the Jews. Now God was telling Peter that the news should be passed on to everyone.

Response
- Hold a quiz on the Bible story.

- Divide a board into nine sections, with animals and numbers in each section. Number the sections from 1 to 9. Score points by throwing a foam ball at the board.

- Paint a cartoon strip of the story on an old sheet.

PETER'S ESCAPE FROM PRISON

Bible base
Acts 12:6–19.

Teaching point
God answers prayer.

Introduction
Get Unknotted: In groups of no more than seven, stand the children in tightly packed circles. Everyone stretches their arms out across the circle and takes hold of two other hands at random. The group then work together to untangle themselves without letting go of any hands.

Link
Point out that it was tricky to get free from the tangle, but it would have been even more difficult, if not impossible, to get free if they had really been tied up or imprisoned.

Main input
Tell the story of Peter's escape (Acts 12:6–19), using a story-roll. Alternatively, you could show either the episode entitled 'Escape' from *On Fire!*, or 'The one that got away' from *Shipshapes*.

Application
Discuss the sorts of things people pray about Ask the children whether God has ever answered one of their prayers. Be prepared to give a personal example of answered prayer. Then write some prayers on strips of paper, and loop the strips together to make a paper chain.

Response
- *Sing:* 'Did you ever talk to God above?' (JP 329), 'Prayer is like a telephone' (JP 448).

- Tell 'knock, knock' jokes.

  Knock, knock! *Who's there?*
  Cows go… *Cows go who?*
  Cows go 'moo', not 'who'!

  Knock, knock! *Who's there?*
  Alex… *Alex who?*
  Alex-plain later, when you let me in!

  Knock, knock! *Who's there?*
  Emma… *Emma who?*
  Em-ma new neighbour, just called to say hello.

  Knock, knock! *Who's there?*
  Noah… *Noah who?*
  No-ah don't know who you are either!

  Knock, knock! *Who's there?*
  Anna… *Anna who?*
  Ann-another mosquito!

  Knock, knock! *Who's there?*
  Luke… *Luke who?*
  Luke through the keyhole and you'll find out!

  Knock, knock! *Who's there?*
  Isaac… *Isaac who?*
  Isaa-coming in!!

THE HOLY SPIRIT TODAY

Bible base
Galatians 5:22–23.

Teaching point
The Holy Spirit works in the lives of God's friends, making them more like Jesus.

Introduction
- *Fruit Salad:* Sit the children in a circle, with one child in the middle. Go round the circle naming each child in turn, 'Apple, peach, banana, pear'. The person in the middle calls out the name of one or two of these fruits. All the children called those fruits change places, while the caller in the middle tries to grab a place in the circle. The child who ends up without a place becomes the caller.

- Do a survey to find the group's top ten favourite fruits.

- Have a fruit-tasting session, discussing the variety of textures and flavours.

Link
Draw out the point that one of the jobs of the Holy Spirit is to make us more like Jesus. The Bible describes this as the Spirit producing fruit in our lives. Brainstorm together the qualities Jesus had which we can imitate.

Main input
Look up Galatians 5:22–23 together and compare the qualities listed there to those you have just talked about. Go through the list, discussing them in turn, and writing each one on a balloon which you tie to a tree-shaped piece of card as you explain it. Point out to the children that a fruit tree is no use if it does not produce fruit. If someone is following God, the Holy Spirit helps that person to be more like Jesus and to display these qualities like fruit in his or her life.

Application
In small groups, ask the children to choose one of the qualities listed in Galatians, and to act out a situation that illustrates it.

Response
- The group prays in a circle. Each person turns to the left and puts their hands on the shoulders of the person in front. Together, they pray out loud, 'Holy Spirit, please help [name of the person they are holding] to be more like Jesus. Amen.' Then they turn to the person on their right and repeat the prayer.

- *Sing:* To the tune of 'Frère Jacques':

  Holy Spirit, Holy Spirit –
  He's from God, he's from God –
  Helps us live like Jesus, helps us live like
  Jesus –
  Thank you, God! Thank you, God!

MORE THAN A BOOK

A LIBRARY

Teaching point

The Bible is not just one book but a collection of sixty-six different books, written by a number of different people who were all inspired by God.

Introduction

- Play charades, using book titles, eg *Around the World in Eighty Days, The Sleeping Beauty, Charlie and the Chocolate Factory.*

- *Pass the Book:* Everyone sits in a circle. While music plays, a book is passed around the circle. When the music stops, the child holding the book reads a sentence or part of the story.

Link

Talk with the children about their favourite books and different types of literature. Ask where they might find all these types of books in one place.

Main input

Point out that, though the Bible looks like one book, it is in fact a whole collection of different books, like a library. Show examples of history books, song books, law, biography, letters, travel stories, and so on. Talk about the Bible books which can be compared to these examples. Even though there are different books written by different people over thousands of years, the Bible does not contradict itself and there are common themes that run throughout. This is because God told the authors what to write and his messages are always true.

Application

Construct a Bible bookcase (see p 64) out of boxes and pieces of card, covering matchboxes or audiocassette cases with different coloured paper to distinguish the different types of literature.

Response

Bible Ladders: The children sit in two long lines, facing each other with their legs stretched out in front, their feet touching the feet of the player opposite. Give each pair the name of a book from the Bible. The leader then calls out a Bible book. The children representing that book get up, run round the teams in a clockwise direction and back to their own places. The first one back earns a point for their team.

Bible Bookcase

The Bible is a collection of 66 different books which tell us about God. The books of the Old Testament tell the story of God's people before Jesus came. The books of the New Testament tell us about Jesus and how we can become God's friends. Can you find out which page each book starts on in the Bible you are using? In the bookcase below, colour each type of book a particular colour (eg colour all the poetry books yellow).

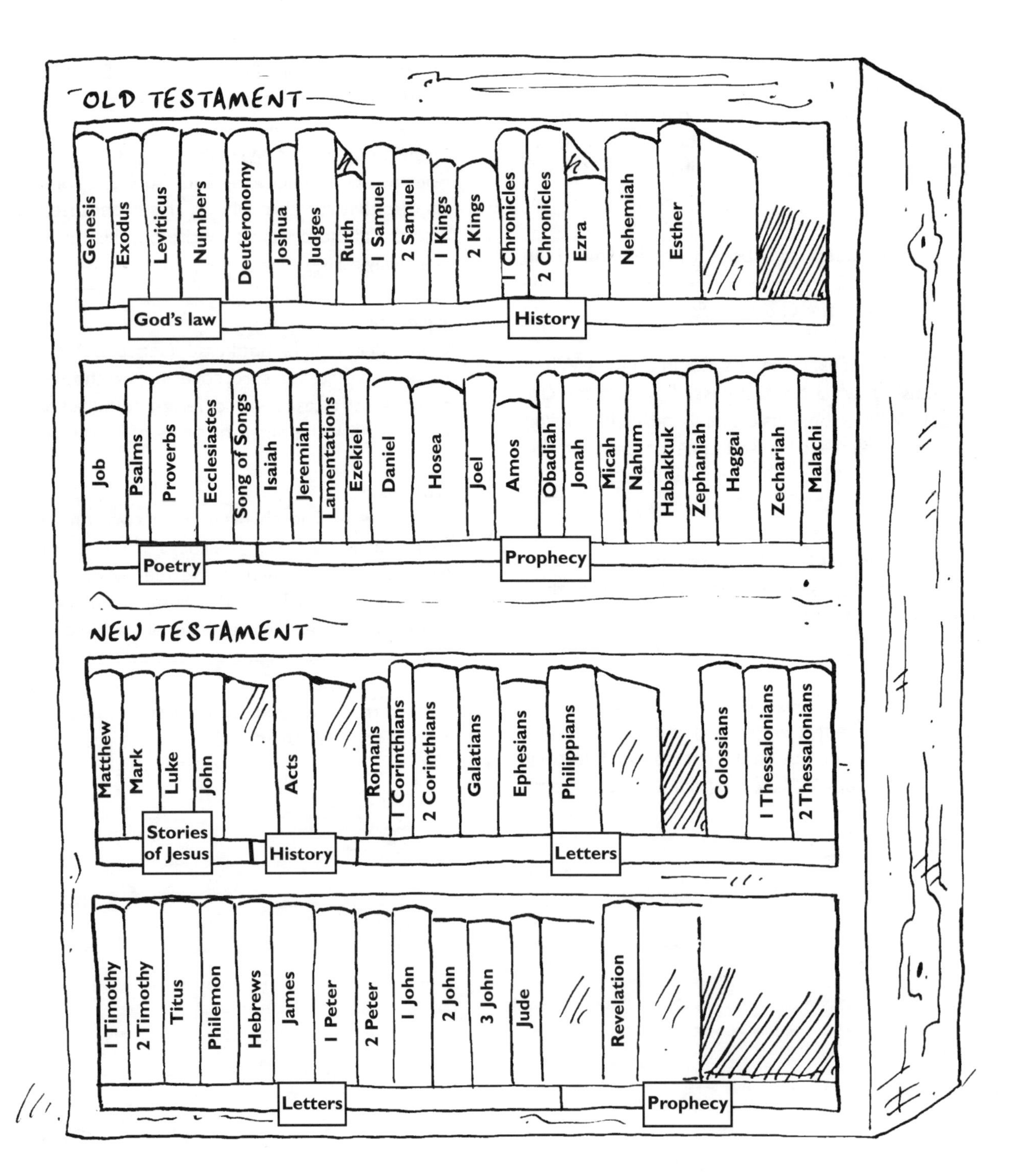

FOOD

Teaching point
Just like food is essential for physical growth, reading the Bible is essential for spiritual growth.

Introduction
In pairs, ask the children to feed each other with long-handled serving spoons. Appropriate food can be things like cereal or jelly. They will need large paper napkins to tuck under their chins.

Link
Hold a quiz on the things we really need (eg water, air, food). Give four clues for each item, ranging from difficult clues to easy ones. Children score 4 points if they guess the item after the first clue, 3 points if they guess after the second clue, and so on. Include the Bible as the last item in the quiz.

Main input
Ask the children whether they were surprised that the Bible was included as something we really need. Brainstorm together what they know about the Bible. Point out that God doesn't just want us to know about the Bible: he wants us to read it regularly, just like we eat regularly.

Application
Get hold of some Bible-reading starter notes such as *Let's Go* starters (for 7–8s) or *Check it Out* starters (for 9–11s). Complete one session of notes together, then challenge the children to go on doing the notes at home.

Response
Using thick card and sticky-backed plastic, make loaf-shaped table-mats, displaying Matthew 4:4.

> 'No one can live only on food. People need every word that God has spoken.'
>
> *Matthew 4:4*

A LIGHT

Teaching point
The Bible clearly shows us the best way to live.

Introduction
Helpful Lights: The children sit in a circle. Go round the circle naming each child, 'Headlight, torch, spotlight…' Then call out one of those items. All the children named that item get up and start running round the circle. Other categories join in as you continue to call them out. If the words 'Short circuit' are called, the children must turn and run in the opposite direction. If the words 'Power cut' are called, they must return to their places as quickly as possible without changing direction.

Link
Discuss together how much a light helps in a dark place, eg in a loft, in a wood at night.

Main input
Tell the story of King Josiah (2 Kings 22 – 23), getting the children to act it out as you do. Point out that Judah had become a dark place not because all the lights had gone out but because the people had been doing wicked things. However, reading the Bible showed them clearly the way they should have been living.

Application
Ask the children how they have been getting on with their daily Bible reading. Ask for any examples of the Bible telling them how to live. Be ready to give examples of how the Bible has spoken to you during the past week.

Response
Work out the puzzle below, and learn Psalm 119:105.

A mirror

Teaching point
The Bible helps us to see ourselves as we really are.

Introduction
The children are in pairs, facing their partners. One of the pair strikes various poses which the other has to try to imitate. Each takes it in turn to be the 'poser' and the 'mirror'.

Link
Point out that mirrors show us what we look like. Ask the children if they think a mirror showing the kind of people we are on the inside would be very popular. Ask them to give reasons for their answers.

Main input
If someone looks in a mirror and sees that his hair is in a mess or that he has a dirty mark on his face, he can go and do something about it. When we read the Bible, it also shows us things about ourselves that need putting right. We can ask God to help us change, and this may take a long time. But the important thing is that we notice what is wrong and do something about it. If you have Bibles available, ask the children to look up James 1:22–25.

Application
- *Sing:* 'The baked bean song' (JP 390).
- *Memory Verse:* Learn Psalm 119:11. Write the verse in mirror-writing, and allow the children to use mirrors to work out what it is.

I TREASURE YOUR WORD ABOVE ALL ELSE; IT KEEPS ME FROM SINNING AGAINST YOU. (PSALM 119:11)

Response
- *Butterfly Pictures:* Put a pattern of paint onto one half of a piece of paper. Fold the paper over and press it down. Open it up again to reveal a mirror image of the original pattern. Cut the paper into a butterfly shape.
- *Positive/Negative Pictures:* Completely cover one half of a piece of paper with wax crayon. Fold the paper in half, and trace a picture on the outside, using a knitting needle. When you open the paper up again, you will have positive and negative versions of the picture.

HONEY

Teaching point
God's word is like honey – it nourishes, cleanses, gives life (energy), moisturises, softens and restores.

Introduction
Have a blindfolded taste-test. Include honey as one of the things the children have to try to identify.

Link
Write out the following verses, leaving blanks in place of the word 'honey':

> He handed me the scroll and said, 'Eat this and fill your stomach with it.' So I ate the scroll, and it tasted sweet as honey.
>
> *Ezekiel 3:2–3*

> All of God's decisions are correct and fair.
> They are worth more than the finest gold
> and are sweeter than honey from a
> honeycomb.
>
> *Psalm 19:9–10*

> The angel said, 'Take the scroll and eat it! Your stomach will turn sour, but the taste in your mouth will be as sweet as honey.'
>
> *Revelation 10:9*

> Your teachings are sweeter than honey.
>
> *Psalm 119:103*

Place the verses around the room, and ask the children to try and guess what the missing word is. When they have had a go, let them know that the word is 'honey', and ask what they think it means when it says that God's word is sweeter than honey.

Main input
Talk about the properties of honey and link them with the Bible verses showing the way God's word can work in our lives:

- Show a Jordan's honey-and-oat bar. Honey gives energy for life.

  > Simon Peter answered, 'Lord, there is no one else that we can go to! Your words give eternal life.'
  >
  > *John 6:68*

- Show a jar of honey. Honey contains vitamins and minerals; it nourishes.

  > Let the message about Christ completely fill your lives, while you use all your wisdom to teach and instruct each other.
  >
  > *Colossians 3:16*

- Show honey-and-lemon throat tablets or honey bubble bath. Honey is a mild antiseptic and cleanser.

  > It is better to trust the Lord for protection
  > than to trust anyone else…
  >
  > *Psalm 118:8*

- Show honey hand-and-body lotion or hair conditioner. Honey moisturises, softens and conditions; it restores.

  > The Law of the Lord is perfect; it gives
  > us new life.
  >
  > *Psalm 19:7*

Application
Invite the children to make cards in the shape of a honey-pot or hexagon (a honeycomb). Let them choose one of the verses that have been talked about in this session, and write it on the card. They can then decorate the cards and keep them as bookmarks in their Bibles, to remind them that God's word is like honey.

Response
Eat bread and honey together.

SEEDS

Teaching point

Although the Bible is like all the things we have considered, how we respond to its message depends on us.

Introduction

Hold a quiz on all the sessions in this series. Keep score by adding a piece to a picture each time a question is answered correctly. The finished picture shows a growing plant.

Link

Make the point that the Bible will be no more special than any other book unless we put into practice what we read. Jesus told a story about people's different reactions to hearing God's word.

Main input

Tell the parable of the sower (Mark 4:1–9). Ask the children to mime the different sections of the story while you play suitable background music. Possible music includes:

- Saint-Saëns: 'Fossils' from *Carnival of the Animals* – illustrating the birds picking seed from the path.
- Rimsky-Korsakov: 'The Sea and Sinbad's Ship', from *Scheherazade* - the seed growing on rocky ground is overcome by the sun.
- Mussorgsky: *A Night on the Bald Mountain* – the battle between the seed and the thorns.
- Debussy: 'Clair de Lune' from *Suite Bergamasque* – the good seed growing.

Application

We all react in different ways to the Bible:

- Some people don't listen.
- Some listen, but as soon as others make fun of them they give up.
- Some listen, but give up as soon as something that seems better comes along.
- Some listen, hear God's word and put it into practice.

Ask the children to think about which category they might fit into.

Response

- Together, compose a rap of the parable.
- Make a collage illustrating the story.

PEOPLE WHO PRAYED

MIRIAM: A PRAYER OF THANKSGIVING

Bible base
Exodus 14:5 – 15:21.

Teaching point
We thank people who help us, so we should also thank God for his help.

Introduction
Make a large frieze showing pictures of people who help us, eg doctors, teachers, lollipop ladies/men, parents, friends.

Link
Talk about how you show your gratitude for the help you receive, eg thanking, paying, giving a card or present, helping in return.

Main input
The Israelites needed help. They were stuck between an enemy army and the Red Sea. Tell the story of how they crossed the Red Sea, and of Moses' and Miriam's song of thanksgiving (Exod 14:5 – 15:21). You could show episode 5, 'The way of no escape', from the video *Exodus* (SU).

Application
Ask the children how Moses, Miriam and the Israelites showed their gratitude to God for his help. Do they think God still helps people today? Encourage them to tell any stories they have of experiencing God's help personally. Invite them to suggest ways in which we can show our gratitude.

Response
- *Sing:* 'God is so good' (JP 53), 'Thank you, Lord, for this fine day' (JP 232), 'Thank you, Jesus' (JP 235).

- Make tambourines by attaching bottle-tops to the edge of paper plates. Write 'Thank you, God' in the centre of the plate, and decorate it.

- Have a time of prayer. The leader starts with 'Thank you, God, for...'; any children who wish to may add an ending to the sentence.

- *Spot the Difference:* Do the top half of the fun-sheet on p 73. The answer is on p 85.

DAVID: A PRAYER OF WORSHIP

Bible base
1 Chronicles 13:1–8; 16:1–10.

Teaching point
God is the greatest. He deserves to be worshipped for who he is.

Introduction
Display pictures of famous people, eg the Queen, Alan Shearer (or some other current sports personality), the Spice Girls (or another current pop group). The children have to guess who these people are and why they are famous. Some are famous because of what they have done, others because of who they are.

Link
God is far more special than the most famous person, because of who he is *and* because of what he has done/is doing. Younger children can draw a picture of what they think God is like and talk about their pictures. Older children, as a group, can go through the alphabet, thinking up words to describe God, eg 'almighty', 'big'.

Main input
Show the children the picture of the Covenant Box opposite. Explain that the Ten Commandments were kept in it, and the Israelites carried the Box with them wherever they went, to remind them of God's presence. Tell the story of David bringing the Covenant Box to Jerusalem (1 Chr 13:1–8; 16:1–10), using a story-roll.

Application
Ask the children how David worshipped God in this story. Make a list of the different ways there are of worshipping God. Discuss whether these are easy or hard, and why they might be so. Ask the children what sort of worship they think God prefers.

Response
Choose one of these ways of praising God, and do it!

- Sing a song of praise, eg 'God is good' (JP 55), 'Oh, oh, oh, how good is the Lord' (JP 180), 'Let's praise God together' (JP 417), 'What a mighty God we serve' (JP 491).
- Make up a dance to go with a praise song.
- Make a banner – the picture next to Psalm 95 in illustrated versions of the *Good News Bible* may help.
- Compose a rap or write a poem.
- In block letters, write out a phrase from 1 Chronicles 16:23–36 and illustrate it.

Spot the difference

Can you find the ten differences between the two dancing girls?

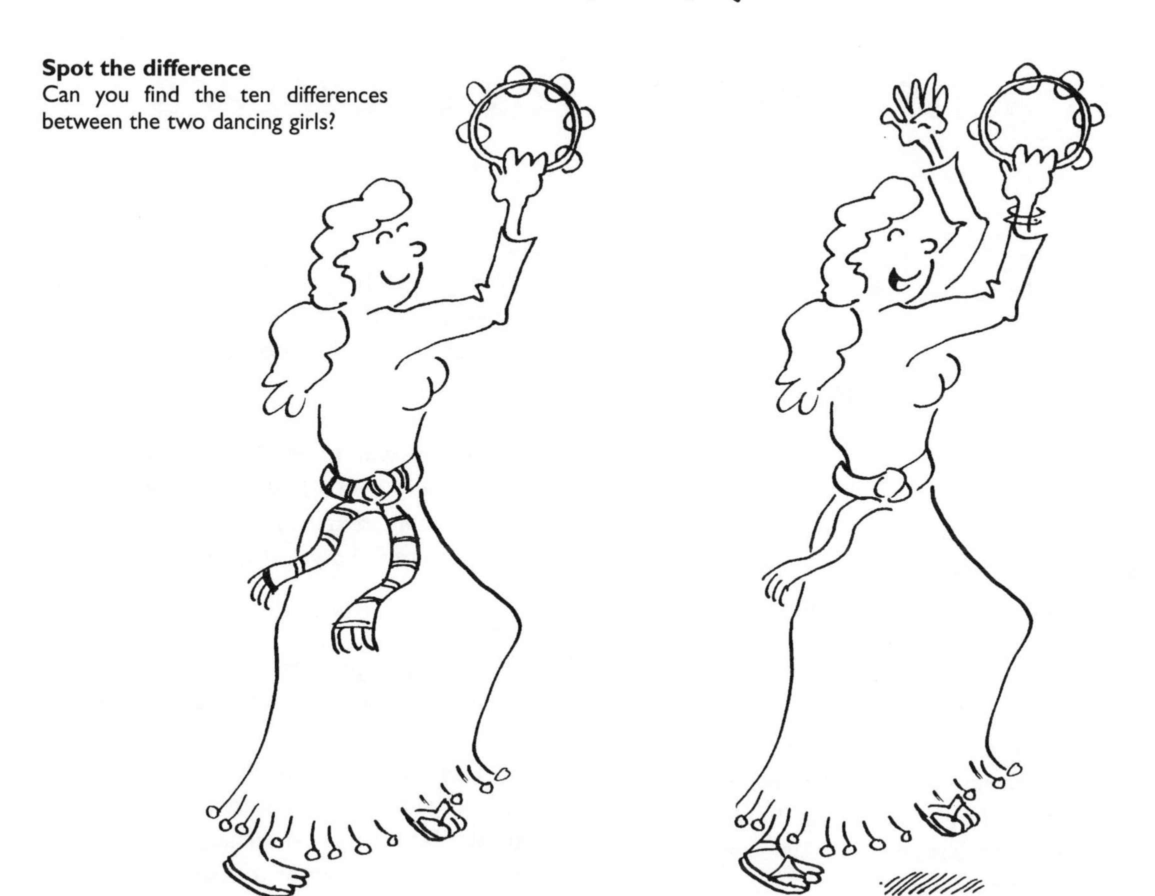

The Covenant Box

This was a symbol of God's presence with his people. It was a wooden box, covered with gold. On top were two cherubs, and inside were the Ten Comandments, written on two stone slabs.

PSALM 139: A PRAYER FOR OURSELVES

Bible base
Psalm 139:1–5,23–24.

Teaching point
God knows all about us, so we can bring our requests to him.

Introduction
Make 'passports' together. Each child draws a self-portrait in one corner, and lists his name, address, date of birth, hobbies, things good at, ambitions, and so on.

Link
Look at the passports you have made. Hopefully, they should all be different, showing that we are all individuals. No one knows everything there is to know about someone else, but the Bible says that God knows us all completely.

Main input
Give each child a lump of playdough. Allow a minute or two to get over the initial excitement, then read the verses from Psalm 139, asking the children to make with the playdough something that strikes them as they hear the reading. Read the verses a couple of times, pausing between each reading. When the children seem ready, ask whether anyone would like to show what they have made with the playdough. Allow a time for sharing.

Application
The psalmist says that God knows everything about us. He knows the things we want, he knows the things we need and he knows what is best for us. He knows the things that bother us and make us anxious or afraid. We can talk to God about anything and he will understand. That doesn't mean that he will give us anything we ask for, because he knows that some things won't be good for us or won't be good for us *yet*.

Response
- *Sing:* 'Did you ever talk to God above?' (JP 329), 'Prayer is like a telephone'(JP 448).

- Use Prayer no. 43, based on Psalm 139, from *One Hundred and One Ideas for Creative Prayers* by Judith Merrell (SU). Alternatively, allow the children to pray silently to God about anything they wish to.

- Ask each child to draw a picture of themselves. Stick the pictures into a book, leaving space to write under each picture. If the children have anything they would like prayer for, they can write it under the picture. Keep the book to continue adding to.

PAUL: A PRAYER FOR OTHERS

Bible base
I Timothy 2:1–4.

Teaching point
Although God wants us to talk to him about ourselves, it is also important to pray for other people.

Introduction
General Post: Divide the children into four teams. Each team goes to a corner of the room, and each corner is given the name of a city (eg London, Bristol, Manchester, Newcastle). Then the leader calls out, 'A letter is going from … to…' The players representing those two towns change places. Vary the game as follows: if the leader calls out, 'A letter is going…', the players walk; if 'a postcard is going…', they hop; if 'an email is going…', they jump; if 'a fax is going…', they run.

Link
Talk about what you do when you get a letter: you open it, you read it, you tell people about it. Explain that one of the first followers of Jesus, a man called Paul, sent lots of letters to help people understand what it meant to be a Christian. Some of those letters form part of the Bible, so they still help people nowadays. Tell the children that the group is going to look at something Paul wrote to a young man called Timothy.

Main input
Pretend to be Timothy, opening the day's post:

> 'Ah, and here's a letter from my friend Paul. He is always full of advice about how to live God's way. I wonder what he is going to say today…?'

Open the envelope and take out a piece of paper on which you have previously written out the verses from I Timothy 2:1–4.

Application
Ask the children whether they think Timothy was surprised at Paul's advice. Why did Paul think it was important to pray for all people? Make two lists of (1) the sorts of people the children could pray for, and (2) the kinds of things they could pray for those people. Discuss what makes it easier or more difficult to pray for others.

Response
- Put around the room cards with categories of people to pray for, eg the Queen, the Prime Minister and government, families, friends, homeless people, hungry people, sick people. Invite the children to go around individually, stopping to pray by each card before moving on to the next.

- *Sing:* 'Everyone in the whole wide world' (JP 333).

ELIJAH: A PRAYER FOR THE SICK

Bible base
1 Kings 17:17–24; James 5:14–15.

Teaching point
God has the power to heal sick people. He wants us to ask him to heal them.

Introduction
King for a Minute: One of the children is chosen to be king. The king gives (reasonable) orders to the rest of the group, which they have to obey. After a minute, another king is chosen.

Link
Ask for suggestions as to who is the most powerful person in the world. Take a vote on it. Talk about what that person's power enables him to do, what he is unable to do. In today's story, we see God has the power to do things no ordinary person could do.

Main input
Tell the story of Elijah and the widow (1 Kings 17:17–24). The children could act it out in small groups.

Application
Ask the children what they think the widow felt when her son became ill and then died. What did Elijah think? What did the widow and Elijah think when God answered Elijah's prayer? Discuss together what this incident teaches us about God. Talk about whether or not God always heals sick people when someone prays for them, and ask the children why they think that might be.

Response
- *Memory Verse:* Learn James 5:14–15. Write the verse on the inside of a get-well card, fold it into quarters and tear off a corner after each repetition.

  If you are sick, ask the church leaders to come and pray for you. If you have faith when you pray for sick people, they will get well.

  James 5:14–15

- Write prayers for sick people on bed-shaped pieces of paper. Stick the prayers on a sheet of card and keep it to see how God answers those prayers.

Hannah: a persistent prayer

Bible base
I Samuel 1:1–28; Luke 18:1–8.

Teaching point
When at first it seems that God doesn't answer a prayer, sometimes we need to keep on praying.

Introduction
Belly Laugh: The children lie in a circle, each with their head on someone else's stomach. A laugh is passed round the circle, by saying 'Ha' and lifting stomach at the same time. Anyone who laughs out of turn is out.

Link
Talk about things that seem difficult, times when we are waiting for things to happen, when we seem to be making no progress and feel like giving up. Ask the children to give some examples, eg difficult work at school, waiting for birthdays or holidays, learning to swim, making friends, reading the Bible. Be ready with examples of your own.

Main input
Tell the story of Hannah's prayer (1 Sam 1:1–28). You could don a suitable costume and tell it as though you were Hannah. Alternatively, if there are two of you, you could act it out as a dialogue between Hannah and Eli.

Application
Talk about the way God answers prayer. He always answers, but sometimes he says 'Yes', sometimes 'No' and sometimes 'Wait, not yet!' (The analogy of traffic lights may be helpful here.) Sometimes, God answers by changing us, so that we look at things differently. However he answers, he does want us to keep on praying until we are sure that he has answered.

Response
- Look back at the things you have prayed about over the last few weeks. Some may be things that need to be prayed for again.

- *A Prayer Tree:* Put a dry branch into a flower pot. Write prayers on leaf-shaped pieces of paper and tie them onto the branch. Over the next few weeks, if prayers are answered, remove the leaves, remembering to thank God for answering them. If prayers are not answered, keep on praying.

DAVID: A PRAYER TO SAY SORRY

Bible base
2 Samuel 12:1–15; Psalm 51:1–15.

Teaching point
When we do wrong, God wants us to say sorry. He is always ready to forgive.

Introduction
Play a quick elimination game, such as Simon Says, or Musical Chairs. Don't leave children out for long: once there are five or six of them out, start the game again with everyone back in.

Link
In the game, once you had got something wrong you were out. In today's story we are thinking about someone who got things very wrong. But God didn't say he was out; instead, he gave David the chance to say sorry.

Main input
Tell the story of David and Nathan (2 Sam 12:1–17). David had sinned, and Nathan came to tell him God knew about it and was angry with him.

Application
Ask the children what they think David felt like. What did he do afterwards? What do they think God felt like? Discuss the sorts of things we do which let God down or make him sad or angry, and what can we do about them. Emphasise that God will keep on loving us, but we need to say sorry to restore our relationship with him.

Response
- *Memory Verse:* Learn 1 John 1:9. Write the words on rice paper using icing pens. Ask for volunteers to eat the rice paper as the group learn the verse.

  If we confess our sins to God, he can always be trusted to forgive us.

  1 John 1:9

- Allow the children to write or draw something they have done that they wish they hadn't. When they have done this, they can silently tell God they are sorry, then tear the paper up into tiny pieces and throw it away.

- Play 'Turnaround' from *Theme Games*, by Lesley Pinchbeck (p 115, SU).

DANIEL: PRAYING IN DANGER

Bible base
Daniel 6:1–28.

Teaching point
Daniel didn't give up praying just because it got dangerous. We need to keep on praying, even if people laugh at us or things get difficult.

Introduction
Play 'Cavemen' or 'Sharks in the Sea' from *Theme Games* (pp 122–123). Alternatively, play some sort of tag game where the children are running away from the person who is 'It'.

Link
Explain that in the game, we were running away from the dinosaurs (or sharks) because they were dangerous. Usually it is sensible to avoid danger whenever possible, but in today's story Daniel had a very difficult choice to make. Was it better to avoid danger or to obey God?

Main input
Make models of people and lions from playdough. Tell the story of Daniel in the lions' den (Dan 6:1–28), using the models as props.

Application
Ask the children why Daniel prayed, even though he knew he would be thrown into a pit of lions. Talk about the sorts of things that make it difficult for us to pray. Discuss whether the children think they should keep on praying even when it is difficult or dangerous. What would help them to continue praying?

Response
- Make a collage illustrating the story.
- *Memory Verse:* Learn 1 Thessalonians 5:17. Ask the children to draw around their hands, keeping their fingers together. Write the reference in the thumb, and one word from the verse in each of the fingers.

  Pray at all times.

  1 Thessalonians 5:17, GNB

- Ask for volunteers to complete the following sentences. Strike a match when they start to speak, and they speak as long as the match is burning:

  'I asked God to…'
  'I find it hard to pray when…'
  'God answered my prayer when…'
  'God is able to…'
  'I feel scared when…'

THE PHARISEE AND THE TAX-COLLECTOR: WHAT GOD THINKS ABOUT OUR PRAYERS

Bible base
Luke 18:9–14.

Teaching point
God knows what we are really like. He is not impressed by prayers that sound brilliant. He wants us to concentrate on him, not ourselves, and to mean what we say.

Introduction
Put the children into groups. Give each group a bin-liner, a newspaper, a roll of sellotape and some safety pins. Ask them to dress up one of their group. When they have finished, hold a fashion parade to admire their creations!

Link
Ask whether being dressed-up changed what the person was really like. Can you really tell what people are like by what they wear? Other people only see what we look like and how we behave, but God knows what we are really like.

Main input
Tell the story of the Pharisee and the tax-collector (Luke 18:9–14, using two glove-puppets.

Application
Ask the children why they think God preferred the tax-collector's prayer. Discuss what was wrong with the Pharisee's prayer. Talk about how they think God wants us to pray.

Response
- Make matchbox puppets (see *Here's One I Made Earlier* by Kathryn Copsey, p 18, SU) and let the children retell the story to each other.

- In pairs or small groups, make board games that reflect good and bad things about prayer, for example, some of the moves might have these statements on them: 'Asked God to help a friend who is scared of the dark – move ahead 2', 'Forgot to pray yesterday – miss a turn'. Then play the games together.

- Do the activity page on 'Prayer' from *Theme Fun*, by Lesley and Neil Pinchbeck (p 74, SU).

GOING GOD'S WAY

OURSELVES

Teaching point

We are all unique and special in God's eyes.

Introduction

The children sit in a circle. Leader calls out various categories, eg 'Anyone wearing pink socks', 'Anyone who has a birthday in April'. Any children who fit that category run around the circle and back to their own places.

Link

- Ask the children to create pictures using their fingerprints, adding lines with a pen to make them into people or animals.

- Pass round a 'magic box' (a box with a mirror fitted inside the bottom). Explain to the children that there is something very special inside. Tell them to look but not to tell anyone.

Main input

- Point out that just as everyone's fingerprints are different, so each one of us is unique. We may not think we are worth very much, but God made us just as we are and he thinks we are very precious. In fact, God values us so highly that he sent Jesus to die for us.
- *Sing:* 'You can weigh an elephant's auntie' (JP 501), 'Everyone in the whole wide world' (JP 333), 'I'm special' (JP 106).

Application

Write out Isaiah 43:4a several times on different coloured pieces of card. Cut each card into pieces and place them at one end of the room. Have the children line up in teams at the other end. They must run and collect the pieces one at a time, as in a relay race. The winning team is the first one to collect them all and arrange the words to make the verse.

> 'To me, you are very dear,
> and I love you.'
>
> *Isaiah 43:4*

Response

Older children could each think of something unique about themselves and write it on a piece of paper. Put the papers in a hat, then pull them out one at a time and read them out. The group has to guess who each paper is referring to. Younger children could paint or draw a picture of themselves. Mount all the pictures on a poster with the headline 'We're all special to God'.

Worries

Teaching point
God knows about the things that worry us, and he wants to help us.

Introduction
Hassles and Hang-ups: The children line up in pairs down the centre of the room facing the leader. The leader names one side of the room 'Hassles' and the other side 'Hang-ups'. When the leader calls out, for example, 'Hassles!' the children nearest that side run towards it, pursued by their partner. If they are caught, they have to piggyback their partner back to the centre. If they are not, their partner piggybacks them back to the centre, ready for the next call.

Link
On a graffiti roll, the children write or draw things that people get worried about.

Main input
Help the children to find Matthew 6:25–34 in their Bibles, then read the passage together.

- For younger children, you could read *The Very Worried Sparrow* by Meryl Doney (Lion).

Application
Ask the children to find three reasons why we need not worry. Ask whether they think there are things worth worrying about. Use the game of Hangman to introduce 1 Peter 5:7.

> God cares for you, so turn all your
> worries over to him.
>
> *1 Peter 5:7*

Response
- *Sing:* 'Did you ever talk to God above?' (JP 329).

- Invite the children to sit on their own, and to imagine that there is just them and God, who cares about them very much. Play some quiet background music, and suggest that they talk to God about their worries.

- For older children, you could cut out the problem page from a young teens magazine, without the replies. In small groups, the children work out what each person is worried about and what they could say to help them.

APPEARANCES

Teaching point
God is more concerned with what we look like inside than with what we look like outside.

Introduction
Cut out magazine pictures of different sorts of people and display them around the room. On a piece of paper under each picture, the children list words to describe each person.

Link
Ask the children whether their answers would have been different if they had been told that these people were in fancy dress, or were acting. Discuss whether it is possible to tell what people are really like by what they wear.

Main input
Tell the story of Samuel choosing a king (1 Sam 16:1–13), getting the children to act it out. Alternatively, you could show episode 2 from the video *David, the Shepherd King* (SU). Emphasise that God does not see people the way we do. He is more concerned about what we are like inside than with our outward appearance.

Application
Memory Verse: Learn 1 Samuel 16:7. Write the words out on clothes-shaped pieces of card, and hang them on a 'washing-line'. Remove the cards as the children learn the verse.

> The Lord said, 'People judge others by what they look like, but I judge people by what is in their hearts.'
>
> *1 Samuel 16:7*

Response
In small groups, role-play the following situations:

- It's your friend's party next week. Everyone has bought new clothes, but you have no money. What do you do?
- A new child comes to your school wearing incredibly untrendy clothes. How do you react?
- Your mum gives you a 'hand-me-down' that belonged to your brother. It's perfectly OK – it's just not the latest style. How do you react?
- It's non-uniform day at school, but you forget and turn up in full school uniform. What do you do?

BEFRIENDING

Introduction
Play a game where children help each other. Write out and display around your meeting room a number of different challenges that involve two items of equipment, for example 'Make a hat using newspaper and sellotape', 'Bat a ball fifteen times', 'Draw a picture'. Give each child one of the items, eg a newspaper, sellotape, a bat, a ball, paper, crayons. They have to find their challenge and the person with the other matching item. The pair then both do the challenge together.

Link
Ask the children if they can think of anyone who has helped them today. Have they themselves helped anyone?

Main input
Tell the story of the good Samaritan (Luke 10:25–37), using puppets.

Application
Who actually helped the man in the story? Point out that Jews and Samaritans would not normally have liked each other. Discuss ways that the children can show friendship to those they like and to those they don't.

Response
Get the children to draw a picture of a friend needing help, then showing how they could help that friend.

PEER PRESSURE

Teaching point
God wants us to stand up for what we know is right.

Introduction
Have enough sheets of paper for all the children to have one each. On half the sheets write the instruction, 'Eat your sweet, and persuade the others to eat theirs'. On the others write, 'Do not eat your sweet, and persuade everyone else not to eat theirs.' Give the children a sweet and one sheet of paper each. Ask them to try to do what their paper says.

Link
Brainstorm together situations when friends influence what you do, either for right or for wrong.

Main input
Tell the story of Shadrach, Meshach and Abednego (Dan 3:1–30). The children can make the sound effects, eg an orchestra playing, the fire roaring.

Application
Ask the children why they think the men made a stand. Did it made any difference that they were not alone, that there were three of them together? Talk about times when the children feel under pressure to conform. Comment that peer pressure can be either a positive or a negative thing.

Response
- Invite the children, in pairs, to think up situations where a friend tries to persuade them to do something wrong, or where they try to persuade a friend to do something right. Each pair then joins with another pair to form a small group and role-play these situations.

- Play a game where the children help each other. Divide the children into teams of about ten players. For each team, thread six cardboard tubes onto a long piece of string, and fasten the string between two chairs. The children position themselves at points along the string, and cooperatively move the tubes from one end of the string to the other.

PEOPLE WHO HURT US

Teaching point
When people hurt us, we should forgive them because Jesus has forgiven us.

Introduction
Invite the children to run around within the play area, without touching anyone else. When you blow the whistle and call out a number, they have to get into groups of that number as quickly as they can. Make the last one you call the number 3, so that the children are in suitable sized groups for the next activity.

Link
Using the 'What would you do?' sheet on p 86, discuss situations where friends may have let the children down, and how they reacted.

Main input
Tell a modern equivalent of the parable of the unforgiving servant, eg Steve borrows Mike's new bike and ruins it, but Mike forgives him; Ian borrows Steve's football and loses it, but Steve won't forgive him. Alternatively, you could read *Miles and the Computer* by Taffy Davis (SU). Then talk together about the characters' reactions. Ask the children what they would have done in those situations. Tell them that Jesus once told a similar story. Ask them to read it (Matt 18:21–35) and to act it out. Make the point that God forgives us, just like Steve/Miles/the servant were forgiven, so we should forgive others who do wrong things to us.

Application
Memory Verse: Learn Colossians 3:13b. Write it up on a penboard, and gradually wipe away the words as the children learn the verse.

> Forgive anyone who does you wrong,
> just as Christ has forgiven you.
>
> *Colossians 3:13*

Response
- *Sing:* 'God loves you and I love you' (JP 348).
- Pray together about times when you have been hurt, asking God to help you forgive.

Answer to 'Spot the Difference' puzzle on p 73

WHAT WOULD YOU DO?

When people...

Draw what you would do.

...leave you out?

...break your toys?

...are unkind to you?

SHARING

Teaching point
To look at the way God wants us to value our money and possessions.

Introduction
Hide Monopoly money around the room. In groups, the children run and find one note at a time and take it back to their group's base.

Link
Share some sweets evenly amongst the group. Ask the children to make a list of what they would buy if they had £100. Then ask what they think a person from the poorer countries of the world would buy. Discuss the differences between the two lists.

Main input
With younger children, you could tell the story of the feeding of the five thousand (John 6:1–14). Emphasise that the little boy shared everything he had even though, as far as he knew, that meant he would go hungry. With older children, tell the story of the rich man (Mark 10:17–27). Ask whether the children think that Jesus was saying it was wrong to be wealthy.

Application
Ask younger children to draw things they have got which they can share, eg toys, sweets, bikes, rollerboots. Older children can brainstorm good and bad uses of money, eg buying too many sweets, keeping them all for yourself, sharing things with others, giving money to Children in Need. Write their ideas up on a penboard, listed in two columns so that they can compare them.

Response
Make some sweets or decorate digestive biscuits for the children to take home and share with other members of their family.

FEELING A FAILURE

Teaching point

God does not give up on us when we think we have failed.

Introduction

King, King, We Want a Job: One child is king and sits at one end of the room. The other children decide together an activity they can mime, eg sweeping the floor or washing the car. They go to the king and say, 'King, king, we want a job.' He replies, 'What sort of job?' 'Any old job!' 'Set to work.' The children mime their activity while the king tries to guess what it is. When he says the correct activity, the children all run to the other end of the room. The king chases them and tries to catch somebody, who then becomes the next king.

Link

Show a picture of a child's face with a smiley mouth made out of a red sweet bootlace or a strand of wool. Tell a story about things that have gone wrong with this child's day, eg she overslept, she was late getting ready for school, she forgot her reading book, she spilt her milk, she broke her friend's toy, she slipped in the mud and spoilt her coat. As you do, gradually turn down the corners of the mouth in the picture.

Main input

'Moses had everything going for him as a prince in Pharaoh's palace, but he thought he had ruined everything...' Tell the story of Moses (Exod 2:11–15) or show episode 2 from the video *Exodus* (SU). Point out that God had not given up on Moses – he went on to lead the people out of Egypt.

Application

Blow up a balloon and hold it without tying a knot. Ask the children to think about times when they have felt a failure. If they are brave enough to tell you, write some examples on the balloon with a non-permanent OHP pen. Release the balloon and watch it fall to the floor. Point out that we often feel deflated when we fail, but God never gives up on us. Blow the balloon up again, securing it with a knot. Wipe the writing off the balloon, explaining that God forgives us and can help us. This does not mean we will never fail again, but we can be sure of God's love and his forgiveness if we ask for it.

Response

- *Sing:* 'Father God, I wonder' (JP 337), 'Jesus, send me the helper' (JP 409), 'I'm special' (JP 106), 'Jesus' love is a powerful love' (in *The Bumper Book of Spring Harvest Kids Praise*).
- On paper plates, draw faces that look sad one way up but happy the other way up. Around the rim, write 'Sometimes I get things wrong – but God will always love me.'

FAMILIES

Teaching point
To look at how Jesus would like us to be in our families.

Introduction
Give each child a card with a picture or name of an animal on it. They run round making the noise of their animal, until they find the others in their animal family.

Link
The children sit in circles in small groups. Each child takes a turn at shaking a dice. According to the number shaken, the child then tells her group about her family, as follows:

Number 1: The funniest thing that has happened to your family.
Number 2: The strangest thing about your family.
Number 3: What you like most about your family.
Number 4: What you dislike most about your family.
Number 5: What your family does at the weekend.
Number 6: Who are the oldest and youngest members of your (extended) family.

Main input
Tell the story of the two sons (Luke 15:11–32), using chocolate wrappers as prompts:

> The son wanted his share of the BOUNTY. He joined the SMARTIES set. He became a DRIFTER. As he contemplated the MILKY WAY, he realised what a FRUIT AND NUT case he had been. When he got home, his father gave him a FEAST.

Application
Discuss whether or not this was a happy family and what was done to put things right. Comment that most families are a mixture of happy and sad: some veer more to the happy side and some more to the sad. Whatever our families are like, Jesus can help us be more like him within them.

Response
Let the children draw each of their family members onto card, cut them out and make them into a mobile. Pray for the different members, thanking God for them and asking him to help them.

RESOURCES

Resources from Scripture Union

THEORY

- *Reaching Children*, Paul Butler: the difficulties, challenges and excitement of making Jesus known to children, with insights into the child's world.

- *The Schools Work Handbook*, Emlyn Williams: a practical book outlining the variety of approaches and gifts that can be used to serve God in a school setting.

- *Who is my Neighbour?*, Martin Goldsmith and Rosemary Harley: the points of contact and possible areas of confusion when trying to explain Christianity to people of other faiths.

IDEAS

Games

- *Over 300 Games for All Occasions*, Patrick Goodland: outdoor games, parachute games, silly sports-day ideas, games for different age groups, pen-and-paper games, games with balloons...

- *Theme Games*, Lesley Pinchbeck: approximately 150 games to illustrate a number of different teaching points, arranged thematically.

Storytelling

- *Storytelling: A practical guide*, Lance Pierson: how to bring stories to life, use them creatively, and make them exciting and thought-provoking. An especially good section on reading the Bible in church.

- *Chalk and Talk*, Owen Shelley: visual communication is an important part of storytelling. This booklet provides practical help for children's group leaders, especially those who are convinced they can't draw.

- *How to Cheat at Visual Aids!* and *How to Cheat at Visual Aids! Old Testament*, Pauline Adams and Judith Merrell: people remember 30 % of what they hear, but 60 % of what they see *and* hear. These books contain over 500 pictures each, which can be traced, photocopied, made into stick-puppets, attached to Velcro boards, drawn onto acetates...

Quizzes

- *Quiz Resource Book*, Richard and Mary Chewter: reasons for using quizzes, guidance on how to use them, exciting presentation ideas, photocopiable drawings and diagrams, ready-to-use quizzes, help with creating your own.

Craft ideas

- *Here's One I Made Earlier*, Kathryn Copsey: a wide-ranging collection of craft activities, divided into 16 categories and linked to Bible stories. An immensely practical handbook.

- *Theme Fun*, Neil and Lesley Pinchbeck: a collection of activities and puzzles to introduce 9-13s to over 70 Christian themes. Photocopiable.

Praying with children

- *101 Ideas for Creative Prayers*, Judith Merrell: a collection of ideas to help introduce and explain to children the whole concept of praying. Prayer is not something just to be recited with hands together and eyes closed. Prayers can be shouted, sung, drawn, made and joined in with.

- *Let's Praise and Pray*, compiled by Christine Wright: two collections of action songs, rhymes and prayers for use with under-8s.

For different age groups

- *Bounce*, Kathryn Copsey and Claire Derry: complete programme ideas for 5–7s, with photocopiable funsheets.

- *Springboard*, compiled by Sue Clutterham and Denise Trotter: 40 weekly programme outlines for 7-11s, with ideas for games and puzzles, and clear Bible teaching.

- *Pick 'n' Mix*, Judith Merrell: over 100 ideas to help you create programmes for children of all ages. Ice-breakers, storytelling, quizzes, paper-craft activities, memory verses, mini-sports, experiments, games, prayers, photocopiable artwork.

- *Let's Explore Inside the Bible*, Fiona Walton: two double-page spreads for each story giving interesting background information and a range of craft and activity ideas linked to the theme of the story.

- *The Art of 3–11s*, Simon Marshall and Rachel Heathfield: published in association with CPAS, part of the Age Range Tools series. Provides practical, biblical help for those working with groups of 3-11s. Draws on the experience of CPAS children's workers.

MUSIC

- *Check it Out!* and *Let's Go* songs: audiocassettes containing songs, with words and music on one side and backing tracks on the other, in reverse order so that when you turn the tape over, you are just about in the right position for that song again.

VIDEOS

- *David the Shepherd King*: six action-packed stories from the early part of David's life, retold by Roy Castle.

- *Luke Street*: Roy Castle introduces stories from Luke.

- *Mark Time*: the life of Jesus as seen through the eyes of the Roman army! A fresh perspective on Mark's Gospel.

- *Signposts*: stories from John's Gospel, all aimed at helping children answer the question 'Who is Jesus?'

- *Exodus*: a baby gets hidden in bulrushes, sticks turn into snakes, bushes burst into flame and an escape route opens up across the sea as God rescues his people, all excitingly retold by Philip Sherlock.

- *Joseph*: we see how God's plan for Joseph works out in his life, from the time when he first starts talking about his dreams to the day when, as governor of Egypt, he is reunited with his father.

- *All or Nothing*: a lively and imaginative retelling of the life of Paul, from his dramatic conversion through to his imprisonment in Rome.

- *Good Friday and Easter Sunday*: two beautiful presentations of the gospel accounts, narrated with great sensitivity by Fulton MacKay.

- *On Fire!*: Roy Castle tells six gripping stories from Acts. Children learn what set the early disciples on fire.

- *Newshounds*, *Chattabox* and *Going Bananas*: three videos to accompany Scripture Union's holiday club programmes.

All the above are published by Scripture Union. You can order them through your local Christian bookshop, or from **Scripture Union Mail Order, PO Box 764, Oxford, OX4 5FJ, tel 01865 716880**.

LEAFLETS

- *On Track* comes out three times a year, containing ideas and outlines for a term's programme for a Christian group in a school. Available on subscription from **Scripture Union in Schools, 207–209 Queensway, Bletchley, Milton Keynes, MK2 2EB**.

TRAINING

- Scripture Union in Schools runs a week-long residential course twice a year, called 'School for Schools Workers', which deals with a number of aspects of schools work including running Christian groups. For details, contact **Scripture Union in Schools**.

- The Schools Ministry Network is, as its name implies, a network of people engaged in schools ministry. A mailing twice a year keeps you up to date with new ideas, resources and legislation, and gives you a list of other members. This will help you discover if there is anyone else near you doing something similar, so that you can contact each other for mutual support. For more details, contact **Schools Ministry Network, 207–209 Queensway, Bletchley, Milton Keynes, MK2 2EB**.

Other resources

IDEAS

- *Building New Bridges*, Claire Gibb (National Society/Church House Publishing): practical advice and programmes for setting up and running after-school clubs for children.

VIDEOS

- *Terry Tearaway* (Tear Fund): these videos often link in with issues raised in the *Tearaways* leaflets mentioned below.

- *McGee and Me* (Focus on the Family): relating Bible stories to real-life situations that children will identify with. Each video lasts about 30–40 minutes.

LEAFLETS

- *Tearaways* (Tear Fund): raising children's awareness of developing-world situations, and what they can do to help.

TRAINING

- The Association of Christian Teachers, in conjunction with Scripture Union in Schools, runs an occasional weekend course entitled 'Running Christian Groups in Schools'. This deals specifically with the nuts and bolts of running Christian groups. For details, contact the Association of Christian Teachers.

- Contact your local diocesan education or youth office to see if they are running any useful courses in your area. There are sometimes day or evening courses on subjects such as storytelling.

- Find someone running a similar group locally with whom you can compare notes and get ideas. There may be opportunities for you to spend time working with someone in an apprentice-style role before starting out on your own.

- Are there any schools-workers in your area who could give advice and maybe even visit occasionally to help you with the group? Several national organisations – such as Scripture Union, Youth for Christ or Crusaders – have local workers, besides numerous independent trusts who employ schools workers.

RESOURCE CENTRES

- There may be a Christian resource library near you, so that you can borrow rather than buy books listed here, or at least see whether you are likely to use them before you buy.

- Some diocesan libraries lend out for free and will even post things to you. However, they do ask for a contribution towards postage. Find out what is available in your area by contacting the Diocesan Office. If you cannot find anything locally, contact the **Bath and Wells Resource Centre, The Old Deanery, Wells, Somerset, tel 01749 670777**; or **All Saints Resource Centre, 1 All Saints Court, Bristol, tel 0117 9277454**.

- The Children's Scrapstore: Scrapstores collect craft materials that businesses would otherwise throw away, and make it available for people working with children. You need to become a member of your nearest Scrapstore, paying an annual fee. Your school may already be a member and be willing for you to use their card occasionally. Once you are a member, you can get a trolley-load of scrap-paper, large sheets of card, sticky-backed plastic, aerosol-can lids, rip-stop nylon, for a nominal charge (currently £6). Look in your local phone book to find the one nearest you.